To: Augustus Invictus &,
Sol

D0998825

Stay fierce!

THE FIERCE URGENCY OF NOW

ELI GONZALEZ

I am so honored God has blessed me with friends (family) like you.

Thanks for your love, respect, friendship and prayers.

We love you very, very much!

Che

Stay fierce!

The Fierce Urgency of Now
By Eli Gonzalez

Published by: The Ghost Publishing
Author: Eli Gonzalez
Contact info: Eli@theghostpublishing.com
Cover Design: Ymmy Marketing

Dedication

This book is dedicated to...

My Lord and Savior, Jesus, the risen Christ.

The love of my life, my wife Maria Gonzalez.
I can't ever thank you enough for helping me out of the darkness.

To Alexis Rose Gonzalez - "Lexi" - for staying with your fahzah during my worst times and for helping me find the strength and courage to defeat, The Mask.

And to all of us,
those living in the midst of the struggle
to improve every day.

Dedication

You don't just live once,
you get to live every single day God grants you.

Live with purpose.
Live with passion.
Live to affect change.

Live with Fierce Urgency

Table of Contents

Introduction

I love being alive!

It's not hyperbole and I'm not taking "happy" pills. You have to understand, I was given a death sentence – Stage 3 Throat Cancer, a disease that has killed millions of people. And it nearly took me out.

But, as someone who's escaped the hangman's noose, the grass seems a little greener, the birds' songs sound a little sweeter, and each day is a little richer than before.

Although the process was nearly unbearable... by God's grace, I survived. The problem is, I'm sick of surviving. Allow me to illustrate what I mean.

You can either go through life surviving – meaning, just getting by without ever scratching the surface of your true potential, or you can accept the fierce urgency of *now* – knowing tomorrow is not promised, but doing everything in your power to live a better life.

One night in particular, when I thought I would not live to see the sun shine through my hospital room the next day, I looked back on my life and, if I could have, I would have cried, knowing I was going to die without ever living the life I was equipped to. I hope you don't have to go through the emotional, physical, and psychological pain I did to realize you were meant for *more*. More fulfillment, more success, more enjoyment.

The Fierce Urgency of Now

I lamented the many hours I'd spent frivolously. I had wasted hour after hour, just entertaining myself by binge-watching shows or playing games on my phone. Too many nights had been spent sitting on my sofa, watching television for three or four hours, or going to the movies for amusement. I had spent far too much time doing things that did nothing to advance my spiritual relationship with God, my career, my relationship with my wife, kids, and dear friends. The people in my life are the legacy I will leave. The memories, for those who would outlive me, would have been reduced by me doing time-killing things instead of capitalizing on the time God had given me.

Unable to utter a sound, tears fell from my face onto the white hospital pillow, creating a dampness in which to drown my sorrow. I had very little strength and even less hope of surviving the worst disease of the modern era. The radiation treatment had rendered me unable to speak… so in my mind, I implored God, literally by yelling in my head, for Him not to take me. I begged Him to grant me more days on this earth. I did not want to leave, having never walked in the destiny of His promises for my life. I vowed to Him that, should He find it fit to grant me more time on this earth, I would live with purpose and intentionality.

Three months after I left that hospital room, I traveled to hear T.D. Jakes preach. I sat to his left, five rows up. He turned from the center of a large stage and started to walk my way when he uttered these words, "It's time to live with a fierce urgency of now!"

It reminded me of the promises I'd made God. A promise I've tried hard to keep. However, I realized that, in order to keep my promise, I had to share my experience and lead others to realize the simple truth that their current actions and inactions determine their future – and the futures of the family lineage that follow.

I would estimate there are billions of people who have never lived the life they should. Dr. Myles Monroe once famously said: *The richest places on earth are cemeteries.* He stated that the richness of ideas, talents, aspirations, and dreams have been buried there. Sadly, I find that to be true. I don't want to bury my goals and dreams. I want to manifest them into my reality and enjoy the life I've always dreamed.

I now live with a fierce urgency of capitalizing on my present in order to secure a better tomorrow. It is my hope that, after reading this book, you will feel the same.

What are you waiting for to live your dream life?

If you're married, you know what your spouse likes. How much longer will you go without doing the small, simple things that can enrich your marriage? Appreciation comes with everyday things like a spontaneous back scratch or doing the dishes or taking out the trash without being asked.

How much longer will you despise your living conditions – or your job – without doing anything to improve the situation? How much longer will you continue to be an overlooked employee and not the business owner you've always dreamed of becoming? How much longer will you wish you could play guitar, but never take lessons?

Why would anyone not want to live a better life?

You are the only one who can make your life better. Time keeps on ticking. Every second you waste is a second you'll never get back. I declare there is greatness inside of you, trapped by a mindset of contentment or insecurities. I urge you to fight it with all you have. Strive to live the life God ordained you to live.

The Fierce Urgency of Now

My hope for this book is that it finds its way into the hands of those who feel like they were meant for more. I pray that it jolts them into action that manifests positive change. Mostly, I hope it shows people the God-given, destiny-changing power of harnessing the fierce urgency of *now*.

PART ONE
My Journey

*"The road may be rough,
the journey may be tough,
and the experience may be bitter
but they are stepping stones
to our future thrones."*

Bomaigboye Olurotimi

Chapter 1

Let Us Reason Together

This book will be much more impactful for you if we can agree on a few things. The first thing I want to come to an understanding with you is this: better days are ahead for you.

Whatever issues, demons, sicknesses, or situations you struggle with are not new. Whatever has been done to you, whatever you regret, whatever has held you down spiritually, whatever you have battled with at every stage of your life – is not uncommon to man. Yes, you are unique, fearfully, and wonderfully made. However, as unique as you may be, you need to know that the Creator knows you better than you know yourself.

Better Days

The current version of *who you are* can get better. It doesn't matter where you were born or what family you were born into. You may have...

- come from a blessed lineage of pastors and prophets
- grown up regularly attending church, singing in the choir, and serving the Lord
- been raised in a broken home
- suffered from molestation or abuse in your younger or even older days

- experienced abandonment
- been beaten, mistreated, or ignored

The truth is, you are here, right now, reading this book because God has granted you the mercy of knowing that, in your heart, He honors and protects generational blessings and He also destroys and breaks the chains of generational curses. God's grace is the ultimate equalizer. He lifts those whom He delights in… and He delights in you.

This may be hard for some of you to take in. You might be thinking:

- *Oh, but how I've sinned!*
- *I've been so bad.*
- *I'm pretty sneaky.*
- *I can't be trusted when no one is looking.*
- *I don't feel spiritually strong oftentimes.*
- *I rarely pray or read the Bible.*
- *I'm morally weak.*
- *I'm still too prideful.*
- *I am embarrassed by how prideful and evil my thoughts are sometimes.*

Know that it's okay to feel this way. I'm not perfect either, so I'm not going to judge you or vilify you. I'm here to help restore you and motivate you. I want to instill in you the desire to live a better life in a manner that manifests action that, should you let it, will change your life.

I decree and declare, a mighty seed will be deposited into your mind, body, and spirit while you read this book. Only God knows on which chapter or what page it will occur, but a mighty seed will be deposited in you that can change your life – if you choose to cultivate and water it. Get ready for a breakthrough.

The Past Is Dead

Let's also agree on this: whatever good or bad you have done in the past, is in the past. At this very moment in your life, you stand at the juncture of a new pathway that, should you choose to walk it, will bring you into a closer relationship with the resurrected Christ Jesus.

Whatever good you have done in the past is in the past. Know that you don't get credit for how you...

- used to pray
- were on fire for God
- fasted ten years ago

That past is the past. God's blessings are new every morning.

Understand that whatever a person has previously done, or what negative words have been spoken to—or about—a person, has no power unless someone gives it attention or power over him/her. Regardless of the darkness of your journey, your past must no longer dictate your present.

A new way of thinking about who you are, a clearer look into how to be the person you choose to be in the future, will lift you above your past. The willingness to see the past with a new lens has the power to change your life forever.

DECLARE & BELIEVE THIS
My past doesn't control my present...   **Nor does it predict my future!**

When you believe something, you don't talk about it with uncertainty. When you believe something, you declare it, you announce it as fact, and when you do that with conviction, you speak things into existence. Here's the problem about believing something: if you don't act on it, it won't help you much.

Knowing how to bake a cake does not take away your hunger or craving for cake. Being skilled at driving a car won't get you from Point A to Point B. The act of baking the cake is what takes you to the threshold of actually eating the cake. Driving the car is what changes your longitude and latitude. Exercising that which you know is what initiates change.

You may need some help along the way, and that's perfectly fine. Even the greatest of us have needed help and will come into seasons when we'll need help again. Admitting that we need help is a sign of growth and a mature awareness of one's self. However, it's important to know that when you need help, God's Spirit becomes unequivocally important. I believe that God communicated a quickening in my spirit that is designed to speak life and growth to your spirit.

The last thing I'd like to come to agreement with you on as you start this book is this:

God's grace is sufficient.

You might have heard that all your church-going life – *God's grace is sufficient* – but what does that really mean? It means that God loves you enough to forgive you and to continue forgiving you. It means that God's plans for you are better than your plans for yourself. It means that God's teachings, which you can find in your Bible, has all you need to live a great and fulfilled life.

Inner Core

A focus in this book is about shifting your *mindset*. Just a small shift when navigating on the ocean can make the difference between landing on one continent or another. I believe God works in small shifts. He allows us to digest things, mull them over, come to an agreement with them, and then accept them into our mindset.

True change comes when you accept something so deeply that it becomes a part of, what I call, your *inner core*. The Bible says when we come to know the Lord, we become new creatures. It doesn't happen all at once. Our inner core has fixed, bad coordinates. If we were before, we are still full of jealousy, hatred, a desire for drunkenness, and to cater to our selfish impositions. It takes accepting something in your mindset – a period of consistent thinking – for it to penetrate your inner core.

The way someone is wired in their inner core is conveyed by how they react. To respond to something is different than how you react to something. When you respond, you internalize what happened and you think about it and then you give your response. However, reacting to a person or situation comes from your inner core. Your answer to the incident bypasses your thought process. The closer we get to God, the more our inner core reveals His principles of peace, understanding, prosperity, love, kindness, and forgiveness.

The truth is, while you're still alive, no matter what you've gone through, it hasn't killed you! Take comfort in that. The gates of hell may have opened up against you... but you're still breathing. You've been hurt, abandoned, tortured mentally, tortured physically, passed over, looked over, ridiculed, forgotten, laughed at, counted out, or even left for dead... yet here you are, holding this book. I'll tell you why: a paradigm shift is about to come upon you.

Chapter 2

How I Found Out

I rarely get sick, so when I first got a sore throat, I dismissed it as something that would go away on its own. Three months later, my throat was still sore so I asked my wife, Maria, to make an appointment for me, which she did. The earliest anyone could see me was a month out.

A month later, I met with a nurse practitioner who examined me. After a brief examination, he said, "Open wide, say 'ah.'" He told me my tonsils were swollen, thus the reason I had pain. He prescribed something for the soreness and told me if it persisted, to come back in a month and we would have to discuss taking my tonsils out.

What he prescribed numbed my throat but didn't do anything for the pain. The discomfort in my throat graduated to constant pain and began disrupting my sleep. After about two weeks of taking an ineffective drug, I said to my wife, "My throat has been hurting now for over four months. Maybe I need to see a specialist." A week later, September 4, 2018, I met with an Ear, Nose, and Throat Specialist.

Getting to the Cause of My Cough

The throat specialist seemed like a pleasant enough fellow, but as soon as he visually examined my throat his demeanor changed completely. He put a spray in my nostrils, like a sudsy Afrin thing, and then said, "This might feel weird but hold on as long as you can. This is important."

He pulled out a long wiry device, seemingly out of thin air. Without telling me what he was going to do, he inserted the tip of the wiry device up and into my left nostril. He was able to push and guide the wire-like device, which turned out to have a microscopic camera at the tip of it, to wherever he wanted. As it intruded into my nasal cavity and penetrated my upper throat area, I knew I wasn't in Kansas anymore. The procedure wasn't painful at first, just very uncomfortable.

According to my wife, he pushed the camera in for what seemed like about a foot. I was forced to shut my eyes and focus on my breathing as I was experiencing one of the weirdest sensations ever. It hurt… but it was an unusual hurt, so I felt I could hold it a little longer. The feeling went from weird to real pain and I had to clench the armchairs of my seat as hard as I could. I was about to tap out when he had seen what he needed to and quickly removed the device from my face. Let me tell you, it was quite a surreal experience.

The doctor told me he wanted me to get a CT Scan. It's a procedure where they would inject blue fluid into my bloodstream and take some X-rays of my neck area. He said, depending on the results, I might have to have a biopsy. Honestly, I wasn't worried… at all.

God and My Wife Took Over

Prior to exiting, we spoke with a member of his staff, who said it would take the radiology place a few days for our insurance to approve the procedure. That's when Maria took over and God began to move mountains.

She didn't call the place where I was to take the test, she went there in person, dragging me with her. She chatted up the two women that worked in the office, as if they were life-long friends. They told her I could be seen in three weeks and asked if a Tuesday or Thursday was better for us.

"I'm sorry, I know you see this every day, but this is my husband. I need him." Tears started to roll down Maria's face. "His children need him. Cheryl, (not her real name) I need you to come through for us in a big way. He's been dealing with this for months now. We need this procedure done today. You and God can pull it off. I know you can!"

I felt uncomfortable. My wife was crying in a crowded waiting room and the woman had just told her they couldn't see me for three weeks, but my wife was asking her to arrange the schedule so that they saw me that very day. We had just walked in!

The woman held my wife's hand. "Let me see what I can do for you." While concentrating on her computer screen, she replied, "Oh, hold on. There's been a cancellation today at 3:00 p.m. If your insurance approves it, you can come back then."

"We'll be back today. Thank you so much!" Maria said.

"Don't get your hopes up. Insurance companies often take forty-eight hours on something like this."

DECLARE & BELIEVE THIS
I must persevere and be persistent *to have a breakthrough!*

We went home and, at 2:40 p.m., my wife told me to get into the car.

"Has the insurance approved it yet?" I asked.

"No, but they will. Come on, get into the car."

"Babe, I don't want to go over there for nothing," I argued.

"Haven't you heard?" she asked. "The Devil is a liar. They're going to see you today."

I got in the car, thinking we were going to waste a trip. When we arrived at the doctor's office, sure enough, the insurance had not approved it yet. I filled out the paperwork anyway and, as I was finishing it, noticed Maria had been praying for us. The only slot available for three weeks was that day at 3:00 p.m. It was 2:47 p.m. when I finished filling out the paperwork.

Right at 2:58 p.m., the office assistant cheered. "They just approved it! You're all set!" The two women came around the desk to hug my wife, while I placed the paperwork on the counter. They did the CT scan on me that same day!

The doctor called me the following day and informed me that I needed a biopsy. Again, my wife and God took over. She pushed and cried her way for them to do the biopsy for me the following day! I went to two more appointments that I was able to get in earlier than expected. The last place told us they could see me in two months. *Nope.* They saw me three days later! To the utter shock of the doctor and the women who attended us, I had done all the appointments in ten days. God and my wife were on fire! All we had to do was wait for the results.

There was no way I had cancer; I just knew it. While my wife worried and prayed for me, I kept going, business as usual. I have the type of mindset that I don't worry about something until it becomes real. I don't worry about *maybes* or *possibilities.* It doesn't fit into my psyche to worry about something that hasn't been confirmed. Besides, me? Cancer? No way! Throat cancer? I had never smoked and was healthy. I couldn't even be bothered to entertain that nonsense.

I had a business trip scheduled in North Carolina, so I went. The doctor had prescribed me a pack of steroid pills that helped with the pain, so I went on my trip without a care in the world. A few days after I got back, we got the call.

Death Sentence

I put the doctor on speaker phone; he told us that his concerns had been validated. There was no mistake about it, I had *abnormal cells* in the back of my throat. The call woke me from sleep, so I was still a little groggy. After sleeping very little, due to the pain, I thought I heard some good news.

"Okay, so do we schedule an operation or is this something that can be cured with medication?"

He repeated the phrase "abnormal cells" and rattled off a lot of medical jargon that I couldn't decipher. Maria realized what he was saying before I did.

"What stage is it in, doctor?" she asked.

"He's at *Stage 3*."

She kept asking him questions and, for the first time, the thought that I had cancer tried to penetrate my thick skull, but I wouldn't let it. My wife didn't want to say the word *cancer*. She kept trying to get the doctor to say it, but he wouldn't say it, either. I saw the look of worry and fear on my wife's face and realized something was wrong. I set the phone down on the kitchen counter, walked away, and wondered *what the hell* was going on and why so early in the morning?

A cold chill crept up my spine as I started to understand what he was telling us. I came back into the conversation by interrupting the doctor, who, by the way, had spent ten more minutes dancing around actually saying what needed to be said.

"Wait, wait. Doc, are you saying that I have *Stage 3 Throat Cancer*?"

"Yes."

He still wouldn't say the words, but his *yes* was confirmation enough. My wife and I bombarded him with questions. After a minute, the moment got too big for me, and I stopped talking and listening. I walked away with my head in my hands. I had been given a death sentence, even though I felt I was nowhere near done on this earth.

Thoughts of my impending death ran through my mind as Maria finished the call. I had a fleeting vision of my wife staring down at my casket and a peek of the faces of my children. The same children my wife told the receptionist needed their father. *Are they destined to live the rest of their lives without me?* Then I thought of my mother, who had just had a pacemaker installed. I wondered if news of my demise would trigger her heart to fail – that's when a single tear slid down my cheek.

The next thing I knew, Maria hugged me from behind. We stood in the middle of our kitchen, in silence for about two minutes. I turned and faced her.

I wish I could say that, as a believer in the Living God, I laughed. That my faith took the news and spit on it. That we started planning on how to give our testimony about what we were about to go through. But I'm going to be raw and transparent. We didn't laugh, we didn't boast, and we didn't belittle the situation. Our worlds were rocked.

"What is going on?" There was a quiver of fear and incredulity in my voice. She told me later that she had never heard such insecurity from me before. She was trying so hard not to sob, although the tears had begun streaming down her cheeks. We cried together for a little while. During that time, no words were exchanged, even though many emotions were expressed. It was the most intimate and honest moment I'd ever shared with another human being.

"You know I'll always love you." Her voice was soft and fragile. She buried her head in my chest.

"I may not be around much longer to receive your love," I said softly. We both smiled sadly.

Then, our faith kicked in. We went to the living room and got on our knees in front of the sofa. We prayed quietly for a few minutes. I got up and set up the Bluetooth speaker; we listened to Christian music and continued to pray. I don't know how long we prayed, but it was long enough for us to dry our eyes and remember that God has the final say on all things. That day, September 18, 2018, marked us forever.

By midday, I started to feel better, ignorant of what was in store for my family and me. Had I known I would have cried longer and been much more afraid.

Chapter 3

The Day After
—◦∾⊰⊱⊰⊱⊰⊱∿◦—

My brain was dazed for the rest of that day. It was as if my wife and I couldn't think of anything else. Our faith was solid, it really was, but our minds couldn't escape the apprehension of the unknown. I refused to go online and find out about survival rates, different forms of treatments, or testimonials of people that had lived through it. I just knew that whatever the survival rate was, I was going to be in that group.

That first day was spent in reflection and prayer. We didn't tell anyone. It was for us and us alone. Somehow, we managed to get through the day and see the sun in the sky the next. I knew we had to tell my loved ones, but I wasn't sure how. I never liked being the bearer of bad news, so it was difficult for me to tell people I love that I was diagnosed with *Stage 3 Throat Cancer*. Still, it had to be done. Worse still, I had to do it.

Making Dreaded Phone Calls

I called my son Isaiah first. He and his sisters, my daughters Alexis and Mia, my oldest daughter, live with their mother in Rhode Island. Isaiah didn't answer, but a moment later he called me via FaceTime. He was with Alexis (who we lovingly call Lexi).

"Hey, Pops!" he greeted, with a big smile.

"S'up Daddy," Lexi said. She was sitting next to him but was playing a video game and wasn't giving me her full attention.

"Hey Rats." My nickname for them. "Is Mia there also?" I asked. She wasn't. I figured they would have to tell her.

I wouldn't bother with any small talk. I got right into it. "Listen, I have something very important to tell you."

Isaiah still had a smirk on his face, being that we always joked around. Maybe he thought I was going to tell them something about my work or that I was going to see them. He simply was not expecting to hear what I had to say.

"I don't know how to say this, guys, so I'm just going to say it. And, I'm 100% serious." I had to say that so they knew I wasn't trying to pull their leg. I stared at them on my screen, hating was what going to come out of my mouth next.

"I'm sick, guys," I said somberly.

"What do you mean, sick?" Isaiah asked. "What are you saying?"

"I'm saying... that I got some really, really bad news." I took a deep breath while they waited for me to tell them. I had their undivided attention. "I just got diagnosed with *Stage 3 Throat Cancer*."

"What?" Lexi exclaimed. "What are you talking about?" She had stopped playing the video game.

"Dad, Dad, wait," Isaiah said, trying to get a grip on the situation.

"What does that mean?" Lexi asked.

"It means that I have to go through some serious treatment." The look on their faces told me that they took the news like I did initially, that it was a potential death sentence. "But I'm going to be all right. Your dad isn't going anywhere. I promise."

The conversation continued and I was able to make them feel better about my situation, although everyone's eyes got watery for a little while. It was hard ending the FaceTime call, but I had plenty of such calls to make. I contacted my eldest son Joshua next.

"No way, Dad!" he yelled.

That call got a little more emotional as I didn't feel the need to hold back my true feelings of concern for Josh, who's a young man already. The call ended with him checking to see if he could get time off to spend with me.

Then I called my parents. My mother answered on the first ring. She had known about the tests and had already been praying for me. I was nervous about telling her. We had recently lost a brother a few years before, her youngest son, and I didn't want her to think she was going to lose me. On top of that, she had had recent heart problems and was wearing a pacemaker.

She was positive from the start, "Don't worry, Che. The devil is a liar. You're going to be okay." My father was also very confident that I would be okay from the start.

I then called my brothers and sisters in order of oldest to youngest. I called Jessie, Orlando, Marilyn, Sorines, Steven, and Herson. They each answered the phone and encouraged me as best they could. I then called my brother in law, Peter, Sorines' husband, who had been a best friend to me since I'd met him. He, too, was very encouraging.

After calling my immediate family, I was exhausted. On one hand, I was encouraged because they were all so positive. But on the other hand, I think I was expecting a little more pity. I wanted an excuse to throw a pity party for myself, but no one was willing to help me.

That second day was a tough one for me emotionally. I was torn between feeling sorry for myself and feeling optimistic. I wanted to cry and rant about how unfair it all was, but I couldn't. I don't know if it was my faith that kept me from throwing a tantrum or if it was the support and love from my wife and family, but I couldn't lash out to God about how unfair all of this was.

I had one more conversation to have. This one was with my youngest daughter, Trinity, who was eleven. She is the only child Maria and I have together, so naturally, she lived with us. We waited for her to come home from school and continued to wait for her to enjoy her dinner. As much as I dreaded it though, the time came to tell my baby girl the news.

We sat her down directly in front of me, with Maria to my side. "Am I in trouble?" she asked.

I smiled, "No, baby. You're not in trouble." In my mind I thought, *you're not in trouble, I am.*

"But Daddy has to tell you something and it's serious," Maria said, setting the tone.

"What is it, Dad?" she asked. I could clearly see the nervousness etched in her face.

There was no use prolonging it; so, I started the same way I told the rest of my kids and family. "I'm sick, baby."

Trinity's bottom lip started to quiver. Maria ran to the kitchen to get some tissues.

"I'm going to be all right, baby. I promise."

She nodded and took the napkins from her mother. "How sick are you?" she squeaked out.

"Well, baby, the doctors have diagnosed with me throat cancer," I said.

Trinity's face bunched up and tears flowed anew as she started to sob. She flung herself on me, holding me tight as she cried.

I hated telling her I was sick. I hated telling her I had cancer. I hated that she was crying. I hated that, in a less than 48 hours, my life had changed so much. I hated that I didn't know if I was going to live or die, but the thought of not knowing felt as if I was not trusting in God. I wanted to be anywhere else but there, yet I was exactly where I needed to be.

"Daddy's going to be okay, baby," Maria said, she leaned over and stroked Trinity's hair. "He has to go through a rough treatment, but he's strong."

"You're going to be okay, right Dad? You're strong, right?" she asked, as if her own life depended on my answer.

I raised my right arm and flexed my muscle and smiled at her, "Daddy's strong, like bull." She gifted me with a genuine smile. Maria went with her to her bedroom. The last thing I heard before they closed the door was her telling her mother that I was funny. It warmed my heart.

I sat there, alone, in the living room. The secret was out. Soon, everyone would know I was dying of cancer. I dreaded seeing looks of pity. I didn't want people calling to check up on me, texting me, or messaging me to tell me they were praying for me and to just believe in God because everything was going to be all right. I went outside for a walk. God and I needed to talk.

All Wrong

"Lord, what's going on? How can you allow this? I'm not perfect, but I'm serving you as best I can. How?" My steps quickened, as did my temper.

"What the hell? I never even smoked! Throat cancer? Why?" It was a cloudy night and it was dark everywhere except under the streetlights. I walked only where it was dark.

"What about the company? I'm scheduled to be a speaker at a huge event in Washington, DC! We paid a lot of money to be there. How will the company stay afloat? I'm going to lose some incredibly talented people. Why would you allow this to happen?" My temper tantrum and pity party were in full swing.

"I'm supposed to give a month's worth of leadership classes at church. I'm a part of the worship team. I have books I'm contracted to write. It's just not right! I don't deserve this."

God didn't answer me. Not verbally, not in my spirit, not even through a thought in my head. He remained silent as I railed at Him in the darkness.

"What about the promises you made me? What about the prophetic words spoken over my life? How can they be fulfilled if this thing kills me?"

I stopped my rant to catch my breath and to look around to see if anyone was watching me. I must have looked like a lunatic as I stood in the shadows, seemingly arguing with myself.

That's when it hit me. I wasn't talking to God. That's why He hadn't answered me. I was arguing with myself. Voicing every little fear, voicing every reason why it should have happened to someone else. I had made such a good case that I was even more convinced that this was happening to the wrong guy.

I wanted to yell and shake my fist at the Lord. I wanted to cuss my head off and tell God off. I wanted to bend His will to mine. He was wrong. I was right. I had every reason not to have cancer, every reason not to make my children cry and worry my wife. I had every reason not to die.

"What reason do you have, God? Why is this your will? Why are you making me go through this? I can tell people of your greatness without going through the valley of the shadow of death. It makes no sense."

God has never spoken to me audibly. But in times of turmoil or when I have reached out to Him, I have felt peace or He would remind me of a verse that, while it didn't change the situation, calmed me down and reminded me to trust in Him. But not that night.

I walked into the house, feeling like I'd wrestled with an angel – to a draw. He didn't win, but neither did I. My wife was in Trinity's room. Trinity was crying and Maria was consoling her. I almost entered the room, but I was still too angry.

Before I fell asleep, I thought of the few times God had used someone to speak a word of prophecy over my life. In a way, some of what was spoken had come to pass, but certainly not all of it. It was just all wrong... all of it.

The next morning, I woke up and my throat hurt more than ever.

Chapter 4

The Cavalry

"**W**hat? NO WAY!" I yelled into the phone.

I was talking to my brother Steven who lives in Massachusetts. He had just given me some great news.

"Are you serious?" I asked.

"There is no way you are going to start treatment and not have your kids with you. So, I'm going to pick them up and drive them down to you in Florida so that we can all be with you for the first few days of your treatment," he said again.

A few days later, my house was filled with laughter and joy. Steven had come through and brought Joshua, Mia, Alexis, and Isaiah down to see me. As a bonus, they had even brought down my four-year-old grandson, Zavian. Maria, Trinity, and I were all smiles. The entire family was back together. The house was alive and full of love and hope.

That night, I went to bed at around 3:00 a.m. I had spent the night teaching my kids some card games and reminiscing about their days as toddlers. The best part about it was that we barely talked about my having cancer, even though I had to go to my first radiation treatment that morning.

At 10:00 a.m., my family, including my mother-in-law, invaded the small waiting room at Florida Cancer Specialists. There were so many of us that some of them had to wait in the larger waiting room in another section. It wasn't easy for any of my kids to volunteer to leave their dad, so they would come and go in shifts while I waited for my name to be called.

More than a few technicians mentioned that no one had ever come to treatment with so many people. When they found out that my brother drove my kids from Rhode Island to be with me to start the treatment, they made an allowance for us. Each family member was present when they called my name. I walked into the radiation room with a smile, not knowing exactly what was in store for me.

A week earlier, I had been fitted with a mask. They had placed a hot plastic mold over me and pushed it down on my face and upper arm and created the mask I would need for the treatment.I laid down and they placed the mask over my face. Then, they fastened the bolts on the side of the mask so that I couldn't wiggle from my shoulders up.

The mask was tight on my face and I literally could not move at all. I had never felt so confined before. Once I was firmly strapped in, the technicians left the room, shutting the door behind them. Then the procedure began as a large piece of equipment circled my head, stopping periodically to zap the infected areas. At first, I was fine with all of it. About halfway through, a very small surge of panic set in, and for a brief moment, all I wanted to do was move my head. Before I knew it, the machine stopped, the doors opened, and I was released from being bolted inside the mask.

I was greeted by smiles, hugs, and love as I walked away from the radiation room. The thought that I was going to have to do that treatment thirty-four more times briefly nagged at me. We were all soon laughing and talking as our big, loud party left the center.

DECLARE & BELIEVE THIS

**I can face anything in life
with Christ and my team!**

Later that day, I went to my first chemotherapy session. Like the creation and fitting of the mask, I had previously had a port stuck into my chest. *The purpose of the port was to be injected there every time I went for chemo treatment, instead of a vein in the arm or wrist. For those of us who are deathly afraid of needles, it's much easier to have a port because it limits the number of times you get injected with a needle.*

The chemotherapy, in and of itself, was literally a leisurely experience. They brought me to a large room filled with comfortable recliners. They sat me down and put the chemo medicine into my body through an IV. The treatment was so easy that my wife had even brought me food while I was there, which I ate right then and there. Again, there were too many of us, so my wife graciously allowed my kids to be by my side during the treatment, being that they were only there for a few days. After three and a half hours, I was finished.

That night, we went out to eat. We were in such a festive mood because we were all together again that my daughters sang Karaoke. Then my oldest, Joshua, sang Karaoke. He got so into the song, it was magical moment for all of us. *(I have a video of it, if you know me or if I get the pleasure of meeting you, ask to see it. I promise you, you'll crack up!)* I got to bed at about 3:00 a.m. again. I had made it a point to make great memories with my kids, not knowing how many more chances I would get.

A couple days later, my kids got in Steven's SUV and they drove back home. However, Lexi chose to stay with me to keep me company during the seven-week treatment. My heart was overcome with emotion to know that my eighteen-year-old daughter would rather be with her sick old man instead of doing what eighteen-year-olds typically do.

With the house settling back to normal, I knew in my heart that I was about to walk into the valley of the shadow of death. I braced myself with prayer and a strong positive outlook. The radiation doctor had told me that some people don't have too many issues going through the treatment and, because I was relatively young and in shape, that there was a good chance I would go through it easier than most. I'm an optimistic thinker, so I received those words, not realizing how dark the shadow of death would get.

Chapter 5

Battling Cancer

A week later, there was no laughter. No smiles. No jokes. The innocent little treatments had started to turn into one big nightmare.

It got more and more difficult for me to willingly put myself under the mask. A severe case of claustrophobia had crept up on me and I'd started to get panic attacks. As soon as the technicians would leave the room and I'd be alone with the loud machine that circled my head and penetrated my throat with lasers, I would start to freak out. I wanted to get up, move my shoulders, and squirm around, but I couldn't.

Wearing That Mask

The results of the radiation began to take their toll on the inside of my throat. The pain in my throat jumped to a pain level 10 out of 10. The inside of my throat was completely raw; I couldn't eat or swallow anything. My wife made an appointment for me to get fitted with a feeding tube. *(A feeding tube is literally a long round tube that gets surgically implanted into your stomach. The way a person "eats" with it is by pouring a nutritional supplement – such as an Ensure or a Jevity – into a large syringe that attaches to the tube.)* I woke up from that surgery in an incredible amount of pain. So much so that they had to administer double the regular adult dose of morphine for the pain to subside.

Slowly, everything in my life had faded from my radar – my church, my career, the projects I was working on, my sports interests, my diet, my need for entertainment... everything! My life shrunk to fit only my treatments and my care at home. The mask-phobia had swallowed up every concern and interest I had. I would worry about it when I woke up and I would worry about it as soon as a treatment ended, knowing I would have to get under it again.

About two weeks into the treatment, I met with the radiation doctor. "Doc, what are we going to do about that mask?" I asked.

"What about it?"

"I don't know how much longer I can willingly force myself to get under it. Please, tell me there's another way of treating me."

"Eli, this is the only treatment that's going to save your life," he said. "There's no way around it."

I didn't say anything. However, I seriously considered telling him that I'd take my chances, so great was my fear of the mask.

"I'll tell you what I can do, I'll prescribe some anxiety medication for you. Take it before coming to your treatments. That will help you. I promise."

The next day, I took two pills and my head was floating on air while my body felt like it was ready for sleep. I put myself under the mask and got through another round of treatment, just barely. As I was starting to get used to the pills, things got worse.

Worst Days of My Life

After a few weeks, I had been given enough chemotherapy that, for two or three days following a treatment, I would throw up. There was a stark difference in how I vomited before when I would get sick, compared to how I would vomit induced by the chemo. I had never experienced projectile vomiting before. It would have been cool if it hadn't been so painful and so often. It felt to me that I would spend a quarter of the day in the bathroom, either throwing up or recovering from throwing up. It was awful.

What made matters worse was that most of the times I vomited, I would dry heave to the point where I began to throw up the acidic bile from my empty stomach. When the acid would touch the inside of my raw throat, the pain was nearly unbearable. Things worsened when I couldn't hold anything down, even the pills to help with the nausea or the pain! I would have to just bear the pain for the two or three days without any medication. I was going through hell.

There were times when I thought I was going to die. I was dropping weight quickly and running out of strength even faster. I got so weak that I had to go to some of my treatments in a wheelchair.

"Eli, you're really milking this sympathy thing now." My doctor joked about it. "What are you doing in a wheelchair? I have patients who are eighty years old and they've never come in in a wheelchair!"

Right when I didn't think things could get any worse, I started to get extremely constipated. The doctor had prescribed some laxatives to take, but even though my wife picked them up from the pharmacy,

I hadn't taken them. I had never had a problem going to the bathroom, so I hadn't known what to expect.

One day, I sat down on the toilet, thinking I would go, just like I had gone for fifty years, when I realized something different was going on. I had the urge to go but somehow there was a bottleneck somewhere and nothing was coming out. I won't get into the details of that awfully painful time but will say that I didn't get off the toilet until forty minutes later. I had never experienced that type of pain before. There was so much blood in the toilet that I thought I had dropped my liver in there!

My throat was raw. I was painfully constipated, I would throw up for three-day stretches. I couldn't talk or eat. I was hopped up on medication. But none of that put together could have compared to what the mask did to my psyche. It restricted my face so I couldn't even open my mouth more than the slight opening it had. Had I known how restricted I would feel, I would have had my mouth wide open when I got fitted for the mold.

My biggest fear was the mornings when I had thrown up and had to go to radiation treatment already feeling nauseated. I thought, inevitably, I would vomit during the treatment and nobody would find out in time. During the treatment, I would be the only one in the room, and the machine that circled me and filled my throat with lasers was very loud. I wondered how attentive the technicians were to me. Their voices could be heard while I was in the waiting room while others were being treated. If they did that when others were in the treatment room, they would surely act just as nonchalant when I was in there.

If I were to spit up or throw up, I would be in a dire situation since I couldn't sit up, move my head to the side, or even open my mouth wide to take in more air! My biggest fear was choking on my own spit and vomit. What really petrified me was the debilitating thought, one that continued to sneak past my faith, that I would suffocate on my own spit and vomit and die before any help came. It had gotten so difficult and painful for me to talk that I saved my few daily words for the next time I saw the doctor.

"Doc, I can't do the mask anymore. I'll still take the treatment. I'll stay still, I promise." I whispered with as much urgency as I could muster while hopped up on anxiety pills and pain medication.

"Eli, the mask is protecting you. The lasers are precision-focused on the affected areas of your throat. If you were to cough or even sneeze, even though you wouldn't want to move, you're going to move. If you move, the laser could slice into other parts of your throat and give you a bigger problem. The laser could also slice your vocal cords. So, the mask stays. I'm sorry, my friend. You'll get through it."

DECLARE & BELIEVE THIS

I will do whatever is necessary
to receive God's protection even when it hurts.

His reasoning was sound, of course, from his perspective. As for me, my heart felt as if it went into a free fall. I was really expecting a change in my treatment. I saw a movie one time when the police came to check on a domestic disturbance and the woman answered the phone and even though she had clearly been crying, she said everything was okay. She closed the door on the police, on her only means of escape, and we see that the bad guy had a gun on her the whole time. That's how I felt... as if all hope had deserted me. Self-pity overwhelmed me like never before.

The next day, I brought up the same issue with one of the technicians. "Oh. Well... I guess I can cut a hole in the mask from your eyebrows down to your chin. Would that help?"

I smiled wider than I had in weeks. "Thank you," I whispered. I was so happy and grateful that tears welled up in my eyes.

The next day, I couldn't have been happier to see a hole cut in the mask. She had kept her word! It was an answered prayer! However, the feeling of claustrophobia was taking on an entity of its own in my head. I started having nightmares of being stuck. I would even wince when a character on a TV show or even a commercial was in a confining situation.

I found myself reliving a horrible pattern. I would go to my treatments, throw up, go through pain, suffer from insomnia, suffer from claustrophobia, and suffer from constipation. The pattern repeated itself again and again. At the time, there seemed to be no end in sight. When I didn't think things could get worse, I ended up losing my voice completely! I had lost my primary means of communication to everyone. I was stuck in my own head, which was a dark place of dwindling faith and mounting fear. It was easily the worst time of my entire life.

Chapter 6

Not Alone

My wife was so much more amazing than I could have ever dreamed. I didn't mean to be a big baby, but to be honest, that's what I became at times. As for her, she was the best and most nurturing nurse when she needed to be. She was also the toughest drill instructor when she needed to be. If it weren't for her, I don't think I would have finished the treatments.

She challenged me, prayed with me and for me, tactfully dealt with my tantrums, nourished my faith, and never allowed me to sink too far into despair. I wanted to wallow in pity and win the argument that it wasn't fair, but she saved me from drowning in desperation. I wasn't myself. I was broken, beaten, and a shell of my former self, but God used her and she saved my life. I can never say enough nor give her enough credit for how she handled the many different faces I would wear.

Surrounded by My Support Team

Lexi kept me company at every chemo session. We would talk about everything under the sun until I couldn't speak anymore, so we played cards. She also went to nearly every radiation treatment with me. I've always tried to lead my kids by example, but there were a few times when I confided in her about how scared I really was. She responded by either making me smile or by encouraging me. She always filled me with confidence and reminded me about the many reasons to fight through the pain and fear.

My mother-in-law was also amazing in how accommodating she was. For whatever reason, I only found her bed to be comfortable enough to sleep in! With grace and understanding, she would give up her bed for me and sleep on the sofa or on the recliner she had in her room. My brother-in-law, Pastor Joe, was also there for me more than I can remember. Every time he would visit me, he would pray for me. He even took me to some of my treatments. At times, he would visit, but I wouldn't see him because he would make sure my wife didn't wake me from my sleep. It was comforting to know that in a sense, he watched over me.

My parents were also amazing in their support for me. As was my sister, Sorines, and her husband – my best friend, Peter Lopez. Peter would motivate me to get out of the house. We would either go for a walk around the block or go to the beach and bask in the beauty of the ocean. They made the three-hour trip to see me more than I thought they should have. Just about every weekend, either one or all of them were at my house encouraging me to fight on and laying hands on me in prayer.

My other siblings were incredibly supportive as well. My sister, Marilyn, came to visit me. When she visited, we watched a sermon I had preached about recovery. Tears rolled down my face as I saw a healthy me telling the cancer-riddled me that God has the power to fully recover whatever has been taken from you. I already mentioned that my brother Steven came to visit and brought my kids down to be with me when I started the treatment. My brother, Herson, was going to come see me, but I had an event in Washington D.C., so I asked him to take my place there instead, which he graciously did. My brother, Jessie, the oldest, is an incredible musician for the Lord. We had a conversation in which I told him that I would love it if he walked into my house singing a particular song. He lives in Michigan. I'm in Florida. Well, my siblings, including my other brother Orlando, all pitched in and paid for his flight. Sure enough, on a Saturday morning, the doorbell rang, and I looked up from the sofa and Jessie walked into my house. Jessie had his guitar and was singing that song! It was impossible for me to not be overcome with emotion. Unfortunately, I was too sick to enjoy his visit. Though I was too weak and mostly slept while he visited, the fact that he showed up was more than enough.

One time, Pastor Matthew Thompson from Jubilee Church in Boston called to pray for me. He had done that a few times, but at this particular time, I couldn't speak at all. It didn't deter him; he spoke with my wife. I was able to hear him via speakerphone and jot down a few words on a pad. My wife relayed my thanks to him.

Because I was nearly incoherent, unable to speak, and in a great deal of pain, he evoked a powerful petition over me. I hope I can properly describe how I felt at that moment... there I was, unable to lift a prayer for myself, and this man whom I had only met once and who lived thousands of miles away, called me to lift a prayer up for me. It was a humbling, touching, and powerful showcase of brotherhood and faith in God.

A week after my diagnosis, I created a video and posted it on Facebook regarding my diagnosis. In a matter of a week, it had nearly ten-thousand views! I was inundated with calls, texts, comments, and private messages. When I was first diagnosed, I didn't think I would want any of that. However, I had a change of heart when I realized many people genuinely wanted to support me through my journey. So I started a Facebook page. To my surprise, more than five-hundred people chose to follow me on my journey in the first week! It was extremely humbling and comforting to know that God had given me favor with so many people.

When my health would allow it, I would write updates about my journey through that page. Every post was met with hundreds of replies and responses. People sent me verses, anti-cancer food recipes, uplifting songs, and words of encouragement. The more I shared, the more people told me how brave I was and how much of an inspiration I was to them.

I often felt like a fraud because of the numerous times that I was scared and didn't feel brave. Someone wrote me to remind me that bravery doesn't mean not being scared; it means when you get scared you don't let it derail or debilitate you. The people in that Facebook page did as much to motivate me and inspire me than anything else. *If you happen to be a part of that Facebook group, I want to send you a heartfelt "thank you" for your support and prayers. You are all very special to me and were instrumental in my road to recovery.*

My Hospital Stay

Even with all the support I had around me, with all the people praying for me and the absolute best wife tending to me, the fear of my own mortality kept creeping its way into my head. At times, I feared I would not make it to see another day. At times, I wasn't sure I wanted to make it to another day of misery, fear, and pain. I fought against the pull of despair, tried hard to be joyful, and devoted myself to prayer and to praise. Trying to stay sane and positive, I realized the truth of a powerful biblical passage written by Paul:

Summing it all up, friends,
I'd say you'll do best by filling your minds and meditating
on things true, noble, reputable, authentic, compelling,
gracious —
the best, not the worst;
the beautiful, not the ugly;
things to praise, not things to curse.
(Philippians 4:8-9)

Just when I was almost acclimated to the horrible routine of fearing the mask, throwing up, insomnia, claustrophobia, and everything else, I caught a fever so severe that I was immediately admitted to the hospital. The fever persisted for forty-eight hours, despite all of the antibiotics and every other treatment the doctors had given me. It got so bad that the nurse told me I needed to take off my blanket and put ice bags under my armpits.

I couldn't talk at the time. Still, I let her know that I was already freezing. In fact, no way was I going to get rid of my blanket and no way in hell was I going to put ice bags under my armpits.

"Eli," she said sternly, "you either give me your blanket and put these ice bags under your armpits or I'm going to set up an ice bath for you and dump you in it!"

I looked at my loving, wonderful, supportive wife for assistance. I was already freezing and couldn't handle ice bags under my armpits! To my dismay, my wife sided with the nurse! "It's either that or an ice bath," she said. I looked around for Lexi or my mother-in-law to help support my cause, but it was 1:00 a.m., and they had gone home.

A few minutes later, my teeth were chattering like never before. I had ice bags under my armpits... twenty minutes on, ten minutes off. And to make matters worse, not only did I not have my blanket, the nurse even took my comfy warm socks! Every second of that night seemed to take its sweet time in passing. There was nothing I could do but shiver and bear it, so I did. The next morning, praise God, the fever broke. Never in my life was I so happy to get a blanket and warm socks!

However, my doctor still did not discharge me from the hospital. He had discovered that I had acquired an infection in my blood. He didn't know how or from where or even when it had happened, but my blood was contaminated. I was one point away from requiring a potentially life-saving blood transfusion. The darkness had fully come.

That night, at around 2 in the morning, as I struggled to find sleep, I gave up. I made a prayer I never thought I'd ever make. I prayed, in my mind because I couldn't really speak...

Lord, just take me. Please, take me. I've loved a lot, I've laughed a lot, but I don't want to go through another second of this pain. I don't want to wake up tomorrow and see the look of fear and worry on my wife's face. I don't ever want to see my eleven-year-old's bottom lip tremble as she tries to make a brave face for daddy.

Please, free me from this physical and emotional pain. Please... just... take me.

And with that being the last thing on my mind, I fell asleep, hoping not to wake up on earth.

About two hours later I woke up in pain. The first thing I thought of was, *Why didn't you take me?!*

As the silence, only disturbed by occasional beeping noises from the hospital, threatened to drown me in despair, I new thought entered my mind.

But, what have you done with the time God had given you?

I started to think of my life but I couldn't focus on the happy parts, the only things that came to mind where the times I had wasted. I thought of all the times I had squandered playing games on my phone, binge watching shows on Netflix, and spending countless hours doing mildly amusing things. I felt ashamed for not appreciating the time God had given me. How could I spend time on stupid, pointless things when I could have been talking to my kids, working on my business, or committing more to ministry?

I thought about my prayer and felt ungrateful; ungrateful for not respecting or appreciating the value of time. I wondered how many people would pray for more time, for a second chance to be with their loved ones, for an opportunity to right their wrongs, for an opportunity to make the most out of the talents they had been given.

Before I realized, I shouted to the Lord, in my head...

God, please! Don't take me! There's so much more for me to do! My children need me! My wife needs me! Please Lord, please... I promise to be better; a better husband, father, brother, son, friend, and businessman. I promise to put you first and I'll do what it takes to live up to the calling you have over my life. Just please... give me more time.

After that prayer, nothing changed in the sense that God spoke to me, He still hadn't. A few minutes later I pressed the button for the nurse to give me something to sleep or for the pain in my throat. Soon after, I drifted off to sleep, praying for another chance at life.

God Showed Up

My wife had called my parents to let them know about my situation. That day, they drove the same three hours they had done many times before, to be with me again. My mother was determined not to be there to pray for me as we awaited the test results on my blood.

That moment was the first time I felt God answered me since I'd thrown the little temper tantrum outside my house, ranting and raving on how unfair it was for me to have cancer being that I had a prophetic word over my life that hadn't been fulfilled. A woman named Carmen Montalvo, who lives in Massachusetts, just so happened to be visiting my parents in Florida when they came to visit me. Carmen was one of the people God had used to speak a prophetic word over me! When she walked into my hospital room with my parents, I was reminded of those words. For the first time, I could recall feeling the type of peace that surpasses all understanding. I was still in a dire situation, but when I saw her and remembered the calling on my life, my fears and self-pity fell away.

I was energized by their visit and was able to leave my room for the first time. We went to a waiting area and they, along with my wife, had a great conversation while I silently soaked it all in. The pinnacle of their visit was when my mother rubbed one of my feet with lotion while Carmen rubbed lotion into my other foot. I was in pain, I could barely talk, and the night before I had prayed to taken out of my misery, but all was right in the world, at that moment.

My parents, retired pastors, but active prayer warriors, had given us, their children, model examples of what it was like to live godly lives. To have them there, along with the woman who had declared a powerful prophetic word over my life, made me know in my bones that I was going to be all right. I knew I had to follow through with more of the process, but I knew the end result would be my healing and God would receive the honor and glory.

DECLARE & BELIEVE THIS

**You don't have to be out of a situation…
To see the end of it.**

My faith had received a jolt of Shekinah glory. *"Shekinah glory" means "God's manifested glory" or "God's presence."* When the doctor came in and told us the test result came back and my blood had gotten better so I didn't require the blood transfusion, my wife was relieved and rejoiced. I wasn't surprised.

I understood then, that God's destiny had been manifesting over me the entire time. It had not escaped me that my mother, who has prayed for me more than anyone, and Carmen, the woman who spoke a prophetic word over my life, had both been rubbing my feet. In the spiritual realm, I felt as if they were anointing my feet for a new journey. I knew in my spirit that my feet were going to walk into territories I had never been to before. I knew definitively, then and there, that I had already been healed from the cancer. All I had to do was survive the treatments. God also led me to understand, it's not the calling that kills many, it's the process. In other words, it wasn't the cancer that was taking such a toll on my body, it was the treatment.

Somehow, some way, God had been glorified throughout my entire ordeal at the hospital. Joy had come in the morning. I was discharged later the next day. Unbeknownst to me, my journey was still far from over. The final ten treatments remained.

The mask awaited.

Chapter 7

Here Comes the Son

Talking to Myself

Despite my newfound faith and courage, nothing else changed in terms of my sickness and pain. The chemotherapy continued to induce three days of vomiting and the radiation continued to afflict the inside of my throat in the three areas where the cancer had been observed.

One particular time, early in the evening, I was throwing up in the bathroom next to Trinity's room. My wife had told me that when I threw up, she would cover her head with her pillow and cry while praying for me. This particular time, when my body gave me a break from dry heaving, I could hear her crying. Soon after, I heard Lexi's voice, as she must have gone into her room to comfort her. I wanted to stop throwing up so badly but I had gotten accustomed to these bouts of vomiting and knew that my body wasn't done.

With tears in my eyes from the process of vomiting and from feeling badly for Trinity, I whispered to my body, "You have to stop."

My wife had bought a book by Andrew Wommack, *God Wants You Well,* which we both read. In it, he teaches that you have the authority to proclaim healing and that you can talk to the affected areas in the name of Jesus and that you would be healed. I felt that

God had already healed me from the cancer in my throat. At the moment, it was my stomach that needed reprimanding.

I looked at myself in the mirror, I was a shadow of my former self. My goatee had fallen off. My throat was scorched and looked nearly gray/black. In fact, the only color on my throat was the red from the open sores that the radiation had caused. The hair on the back of my neck had also fallen off and my new hairline was right above my ears – it almost looked as though I had a bowl cut. My cheeks and eyes seemed a little sunken in and I was much thinner. My legs and arms were like twigs and, although it took a while longer, my little pot belly had also disappeared. If it weren't because my eyes were so familiar, I could have thought I was looking at someone else.

I looked into my own eyes and pointed my right index finger at my visage, "You have to stop," I told myself. My body answered by forcing me to convulse. I quickly stepped over the toilet bowl but nothing came out of my mouth. About a minute later, I was staring at myself again. This time, I directed my command to the culprit, "Stomach, I have nothing left. You need to stop. *Now.*" I didn't yell, because I couldn't yell.

I stood there, breathing harder than normal due to the extent of my vomiting. I could hear the hushed tones of my daughters talking in Trinity's room. I was so sick of being sick. I was fed up with how it had affected my family. Somehow, some way, I needed to regain control.

I put my hands on my hips as if daring my stomach to force me to the bowl again. I stood there and waited. I controlled my breathing and waited. And waited. After approximately ten minutes, I could tell that my vomiting session had ended. I left the bathroom feeling victorious, because it was perhaps the shortest vomiting session I had been through.

"Dad, are you okay?" Trinity's voice sounded far away, although I was just outside her open bedroom door.

I poked my head in the room and flexed my now skinny muscles. "Like bull, Trin, I'm strong like bull," I whispered.

"See, Trin," Lexi said, "Dad's not going anywhere. He still even has his corny jokes!"

Showdown Against the Mask

I had ten more radiation treatments to go. Ever since I had been prescribed the anxiety pills, I took them in order to cope with the fear of getting trapped under the mask. But something so momentous happened that I knew that for me – not for anyone else, but for me – in order to know God had brought me through the process, I couldn't take the pills any longer. (I explain in full detail what happened in chapter 9.)

With a new resolve, I took the last ten radiation treatments armed only with faith in God. With God's help, I stared down the demons of fear and went to every treatment with confidence and a song of praise in my heart. I'm not going to lie, every single time they strapped me under the mask, my heart would race and I would be afraid, but not like before. Once I realized that it wasn't just me under the mask, that I had brought with me the power of the resurrected son of God, I knew that in due time, I would rise up out from under the mask the way Jesus rose up when it was His time. Every treatment session got a little bit easier. Finally, the time came when I had just one more treatment to go.

I was having a particularly good day. I hadn't thrown up and was feeling optimistic to be going to my last treatment. I was prepared mentally and spiritually, but when we got there, the machine wasn't working properly, so they sent us home. As the day wore on, my health took a dive and I got incredibly nauseous. Just five minutes after throwing up, I would be in the bathroom again.

A nurse from the doctor's office called my wife and told her that the machine was fixed so I could go there for my last treatment. When she informed me, I didn't want to go. I couldn't go. I was too sick. I usually got sicker as the day wore on. Going in the mornings was tough because I would start getting nauseated – but going in the afternoon was like asking for a death sentence because my vomiting spells were usually in full swing around that time.

Due to my wife's tenacity, I found myself back at the office, headed to my last showdown with the mask. To my surprise, my mother in law, my Lexi, my mother-in-law's friend Gilda, and my brother in law Joe were there to support me! It reminded me of when all my kids were over and I had started the treatment. With a weak "thumbs up" to my fan club, I walked into the radiation room.

I looked at the mask, which was being held by a technician, and said, "This is it, baby."

Moments later, I was strapped under the mask and the techs had left the room and started the machine. After about a minute, my stomach started to alert me that it was about to expunge whatever was in it. I don't know if I can properly express how scared I was. Then, I hiccupped and vomit filled my throat although only a trace came through my lips. Mind you, this was what I had always fretted about, that I would be strapped in and would choke on my own vomit.

I violently spit out the nasty bile in my mouth. Much of it fell back right on the mask, which, in essence, was my face. My stomach threatened to release much more. I was in near full-on panic mode. If I threw up while lying there, I thought I would die. Fear and anxiety fought for control of my thoughts, gaining ground every millisecond. This was it.

I'm going to die here, I thought.

Then, as if a fresh wave of air had entered the room, I remembered I wasn't under the mask alone. "Stomach," I said as forcefully as I could. "Not now. Hold on." I began the breathing techniques Peter had shown me from a YouTube video. "In the name of Jesus, I declare there is no way you're going out this way," I prophesied over myself.

DECLARE & BELIEVE THIS

**Even during the worst time of my life...
I survived!**

I recalled the many people who were praying for me, the calls, the texts, and the messages of support. I remembered how I felt when my mother and Carmen were massaging my feet. As time slowly ticked by, I embraced my situation. God had shown up when I needed Him most. I knew that in a short period of time, the technicians were going to free me from under the mask and that I would never be under it again. I also knew that my stomach was not going to release any more puke. I just had to hold on.

When the technician opened the door, I was still whispering, "Thank you, Jesus. Thank you, Lord." He took a look at me and, noticing the vomit around me, quickly took the mask off of me.

"Why didn't you yell? Are you okay?"

With the ordeal over, I began to shake. Partly in gratitude and partly because I had passed through a traumatic experience. I remembered the one time I was in a car accident and I got out of the car shaking; this was exactly how I felt after this last treatment. I was okay, but I had gone through an incredibly harrowing experience. I was so shaken up, I never answered the tech.

When they opened the door for me, my support group had created poster-sized signs declaring that my treatments were over. Instead of walking up to their outstretched arms, I ducked into a side room and had a moment, just me and my God. "Thank you, Lord. I could not have done this without You," I whispered.

Moment of Truth

Two weeks later, I was in the office of the ear, nose, and throat specialist. I was done with the treatments, but they had told me I would feel the effects of the radiation and chemo for at least two more months. Even though I was still getting sick and using a feeding tube to "eat," I had already started writing this book.

But this was the moment of truth. The doctor was going to put the camera up, through my nostrils, and check down my throat for any signs of cancer. He was going to perform the same procedure that he'd done when he first spotted the disease. I had proclaimed healing and my wife, family, and friends had all rejoiced. However, the doctors hadn't declared me cured.

I thought I would walk there with a little bit of trepidation, but I was confident that God had healed me. Still, there was a feeling of uneasiness as my wife, Trinity, and I sat waiting for the doctor to come in. (Lexi had fulfilled her time with me and went back home shortly after my treatments ended.)

The doctor came in and, in his usual gruff bedside manner, offered very little small talk, but went right to the camera. My wife held my left hand as Trinity immortalized the moment by taking pictures. The doctor shoved the camera deep inside my face, making me squint so hard that a tear ran down my left cheek.

It seemed as if the air was taken from the room as he took his time looking at my throat. After what seemed like twenty minutes, when it was about ninety seconds, he pulled the camera from my nose and sat back on his swiveling black backless chair.

"I see no signs of any abnormal—"

"Hallelujah!" My wife screamed, interrupting his findings. He smiled and sat back as we thanked God and I hugged my wife and youngest daughter. With them tucked under an arm, I noticed he was still there. "I'm sorry, you were saying?" I urged.

"I don't see any signs of anything abnormal."

I wanted him to say it. "Are you saying that the cancer is gone?"

"I don't see anything malignant..."

"Doc, do you see any sign of cancer?" I asked.

"No," he answered.

"Then please, say it."

He smiled and took in a deep breath. "Eli, I checked to see if there is any sign of cancer in your throat. My examination concluded with my *not* seeing any sign of cancer in your throat. The treatments were a success."

I could tell I startled him by the way he jumped back when I reached out and hugged him. "That's what I needed to hear, Doc! Now please, indulge me, tell me the cancer is gone."

"Well, we need to set up a CT Scan and…"

"Tell me the cancer is gone, Doc. If you didn't see it, then it's gone."

He smiled again but held his arms up in front of him so that I didn't hug him again. "Eli, as far as I can tell, there's no sign of cancer." He paused and looked at my family and then back at me. "The cancer is gone."

We stayed in the room for about fifteen minutes after he left. We laughed and cried and thanked God for His faithfulness. By the time we walked out of the room, I was exhausted. I knew that I had a long way to go to fully recover from the treatment, but it didn't matter, I was a cancer survivor.

"Dad, what are you going to do now?" Trinity asked. It seemed like such an open-ended question. I didn't know if she meant when I was going to go back to our church or when I would get back to work or what or if I wanted to stop somewhere on the way home.

"Yeah, babe," my wife said. "What are you going to do now?"

I smiled. "I'm going to let the world know that God still hears prayers and performs miracles. People need to know that we only have one life and we need to find our purpose in it."

Then, I worked on finishing this book.

PART TWO
What I Learned

"Sometimes the bad things that happen to our lives puts us directly on the path to the best things that will ever happen"

Unknown

Chapter 8

Makes You Stronger?

Cancer

When I was diagnosed with cancer, I had no idea what the journey forward would bring. I had no idea that I would come to know myself in a way that had previously been deemed inconceivable. I had no idea that my faith was about to get tested – unlike anything that had ever happened in my experience. I had no idea how powerful an enemy anxiety would be as it tried to control my thoughts and influence my comings and goings. I found out the truth about myself with regard to my threshold of pain. I also came face-to-face with despair on a continual basis. It unremittingly invaded my psyche more times than I'm willing to admit.

I was in for the fight of my life. It wasn't a glorious battle. I wasn't on a battlefield, holding a huge sword, surrounded by my countrymen as we protected our families against invaders. I wasn't on a basketball court with the ball in my hands, down by one point, with ten seconds ticking off the clock. There was nothing poetic or honorable about what I was to endure. This was a real fight for my health and it tested my mental resolve and my belief in God.

The doctor told me, because of where the cancer was positioned – at the top of my throat and on the right side of my tonsils – it was not going to be easy and I would likely have more challenges than most people with throat cancer. He told me I was going to go through a lot of pain, but that I should get through it. I looked at him and said, "What doesn't kill me will make me stronger, right?"

Months later, I realized the truth about that saying.

What Doesn't Kill You...

Most people are familiar with the saying, "What doesn't kill you, makes you stronger."

It's about time someone called that saying what it is: a big, fat, lie.

Most sayings get passed down from generation to generation because there's truth in them. Somehow, this one snuck through. Here's the truth of it, and I'll repeat it again in this book because it's that important, only one thing will kill you. That's it. We have been born to live a finite time on this earth and we will all die from something.

Trials are Personal
Assessment Tests

Here's more truth: in all reality, most things in life don't try to kill you. Sure, we will come face to face with problems and adversity, but they are not killers, they are personal assessment tests. They reveal who you are at your core and what you believe.

Divorce can be devastating. It can destroy additional relationships. It can severely affect the spouses and children from the marriage. It can be embarrassing. It can make you want to cry for weeks, months, or even years. It can make you feel like a failure. But it can't kill you.

Bankruptcy can set you back financially. It can ruin your credit. It can make you put off plans like which car to buy next or whether or not to start your own business. But although it can debilitate areas of your life, it can't kill you.

Sexual molestation is diabolical and evil. It can make you want to shut yourself off from the rest of the world. It can make you feel unsafe. It can make you feel unworthy of love. It can hurt your psyche. It can change the way you feel about men or women. But as horrible as it is and, although thoughts of despair may linger for years, it can't kill you.

Being passed over for a promotion can't kill you.

Getting physically beaten up doesn't kill you.

Losing your job doesn't kill you.

Being embarrassed doesn't kill you.

Losing a loved one doesn't kill you.

Being mocked doesn't kill you.

Being publicly shamed doesn't kill you.

Losing an argument or being shouted at doesn't kill you.

Being overworked doesn't kill you.

Not being chosen for an important team/committee/group doesn't kill you.

Being demoted doesn't kill you.

Losing your home doesn't kill you.

Going to prison doesn't kill you.

Sure, these things and many other things can overwhelm and demoralize us. They can even change the type of people we are, if we let them... but they can't kill us. Just about every trial in life that you go through will not kill you. You could have gone through every one of the ones I listed and still be alive to read this. You could have gone through much more than what I've listed, yet you're still alive to read this.

Problems constantly arise, people are unpredictable, and chaos sometimes gets unleashed in certain areas of your life, but these situations are not hell-bent on killing you. That doesn't mean we are not under a mortal or spiritual attack. You have to understand that we have a real enemy who is out to lie, steal, and kill. Mankind's enemy, Satan, is out to destroy you. He's out to destroy your family, your career, your faith, your joy, your peace, and your soul. That much is true.

It is also true that he doesn't have the authority to kill you. He cannot create an accident that takes lives. He cannot put his ethereal hand into your chest and stop your heart from beating. He cannot take control of your mind and body and make you throw yourself off a cliff. I don't think he even tries. It would be counter-productive, and one thing we learn from the scriptures about the devil and his army is that they are organized.

When Jesus asked the demon-possessed man, "What is your name?" they answered, "We are called legion."

A legion is a military unit. The fabric of a military is founded upon structure, orders, obedience, and self-control. The demons were not a chaotic group of dark figures with pointy ears, sharp teeth, and scaly tails, nipping at one another and fighting against each other. Those demons were working together – towards one common goal, to torture the man they inhabited.

This story is interesting for many reasons. One is that the demons, though they tormented the man, did not have the power to kill him. Remember that. There is no place in the Bible where we see our enemy with the ability to kill someone. He simply does not have the authority. That's not how the game of eternity is played.

When God gave man free will, the rules were set. Our carnal bodies desire to feel good, to be comfortable, to be liked or even admired or respected, to be healthy, and to procreate. It's in those basic needs where we are attacked or enticed. The enemy can't kill us, but he can influence our will. Therein lies the war!

I want you to understand that you are strong… incredibly so. Perhaps you have been lost, wandering in the desert for years or you have been in a valley in certain areas of your life for years. Maybe you may have been exiled from organizations, churches, families, or associations. You may have even built self-imposed limitations around your abilities, spheres of influence, and potential. But none of that has killed you.

Only God knows when you will live your last day on earth. Everything else, although it can make us feel like wanting to die, cannot kill us. The saying, *whatever doesn't kill you makes you stronger*, is not true. That doesn't mean that external forces can't negatively affect you.

The truth is, whatever doesn't kill you can make you *scared*. Being made fun of at school, while it didn't kill you, can make you not want to go back to school. Getting mugged, though it didn't kill you, can make you afraid to leave your house. Losing your job and not finding another one can negatively affect your quality of living. It can make you lose your car because of missed car payments and force you to rely on public transportation, thus changing your lifestyle.

Whatever doesn't kill you can *limit you*. Striking out on your own as an entrepreneur, only to fail, can make you run back to a job and stop you from ever trying to be independent again, thus limiting your earning potential.

Whatever doesn't kill you can *paralyze you*. Falling on your face, whether at a speaking event, doing some sort of performance, or participating in some form of competition, can scare you enough that you never try again.

Cancer can kill you. If it doesn't, you aren't automatically going to be stronger as a result of surviving. I know of a man who had throat cancer, beat it, kept smoking, and died from a recurrence a year later. He wasn't made stronger. I know of another person who had cancer – but felt that her friends and many family members didn't give her the proper support. She beat cancer but came to despise many of the people she once loved. The struggle and subsequent victory didn't make her stronger.

What makes you stronger is the perspective you gain while going through the valley of the shadow of death.

What makes you stronger is not going through adversity, it's *how* you go through it. What makes you stronger is the perspective you gain while going through the valley of the shadow of death. Getting through it, in and of itself, doesn't make you stronger. Learning, growing, and increasing your faith while you go through it, is what makes you stronger.

The barometer that measures if you became stronger manifests itself in your attitude and how you spend your time. Cancer didn't kill me, nor did it make me stronger. But, going through it made me wiser. It brought me closer to God. I grew closer to my family and friends, and I learned to appreciate the present. At the end of the day, as believers, we become stronger when we rely less on ourselves and more on God.

Chapter 9

If God is With You…

W hat then shall we say to these things? If God is for us, who can be against us? Romans 8:31

Here's the issue: Often, we don't consider God to be for us or with us. We believe that He sees us and we believe in Him… but to believe that He is *with us*? At times this can be a difficult thing.

The spiritual separation between God and humanity starts with knowing that God is Holy and we are not. Right from the start of our awareness of the Lord, there's a division that our subconscious buys into. That's the reason why, when we pray, we beg and plead – instead of demand. That's right, I said demand.

See, we, the Lord's children, should demand the promises He has made to us. Instead of praying, "Father-God, please look after my children," we need to pray with more certainty and authority. "Father God, I have given over my children to you for you to look after. Your Word says that it is a lamp unto my feet. Lord, I affirm your decree that your Word will penetrate the souls of my children and declare that you will look after them every day of their lives and that your Word will light their paths."

If God is With You, Who or What Can Be Against You?

The reason why we beg and plead when we pray is because, in our hearts, minds, and souls, we are not sure He is with us, or better said, that we are with Him. Because He is Holy and we are not. How can we feel that He is with us when we sin so easily? How can we feel He is with us when we would rather do just about anything than read His Word?

When you live a life like that and then you hear, "When God is with you, who or what can be against you?" it doesn't do anything to us, because we believe it's not talking about us. It can't be. We're too sinful.

Courage

I met my wife and her family thirteen years ago from the date of this writing. My wife has a younger sister who has always been very pretty, but also very shy. She would get nervous every single day to go to school. She would get physically ill when she had tests or if she had to participate in class in any way. To be called upon by a teacher was almost like a death sentence for her. Even when we would all go out to eat, my wife would order for her, knowing that she was too nervous to order her own food.

One day, while we were all at the mall, I walked into a store and found a small smooth stone and bought it. My wife thought it wasn't a good purchase to pay so much for just a rock. But I knew the rock held more value than the money I'd exchanged for it. As soon as I saw her, I gave the rock to my sister-in-law.

She looked at it and smiled, sheepishly.

"Did you read it?" I asked.

She nodded affirmatively.

"Read it out loud."

"Do I have to?" she asked.

"No. But it'll mean more to you if you read it out loud."

She waited a minute, playing with the rock, unsure if she wanted to utter the word out loud. I waited, thinking she would just put it in her pocket.

"Courage," she said softly.

I nodded my head softly, but surely, with my eyes focused on hers. "That's right, Becca. Courage."

She played with the smooth stone, turning it over in her hands. We didn't have to say much. I knew how timid she was. Even though I saw her every day, she was still very shy with me, but I dared push the issue a little bit.

"Becca, when you go to school, put the rock in your pocket. When you take a test, have the rock in your pocket. When someone asks you a question, wherever you go, make sure you have your rock on your person."

"Thank you. I don't see how a rock can help though… but thank you." she said politely and sincerely.

I told her, "The rock can't help. It's a dead, smooth object. It can't come to life, it isn't an elixir you can drink and not be afraid, and it's not a magic wand that will allow you to escape situations you aren't comfortable with.

"However, courage can. Just for you to know that wherever you go, you are bringing a little bit of courage with you, if you can change your mindset from being alone to being accompanied by courage, that can be a life-changer."

DECLARE & BELIEVE THIS

Fear is real...
That's why God invented courage!

Rebecca brought that rock with her every day to school. As the years passed, she got to the point that she no longer needed to have it with her as she slowly emerged from her self-imposed shell. As I write this, she's a newly-married college graduate that moved to a new state to start a new life with her husband. I could never have imagined the shy Rebecca I met would move away from her family to strike out on her own.

I remember asking her where the rock was about a year and a half after I'd given it to her. She shrugged as if she didn't know. Then she reached into her left pocket and pulled it out. It had become such a habit to bring courage with her, she didn't even realize it when she did.

And that is how it is with God and us. God's presence was gifted to us, as I gave the rock to her. There are times when things happen to us and we don't feel connected to God, so when we hear, "When God is with us, who can be against us?" We don't bank on that promise.

But the truth is, once you've accepted God's mercy and grace and become one of his children – like the courage rock that accompanied my sister-in-law everywhere she went, even when she didn't think it did, so does God go with us.

You have to believe that it's not up to your being holy for God to be with you. God is going to be on your side whether you know it or not. Not only on days that you feel you haven't sinned. He will be with you every day of your life. That's His promise.

God is with you. And when God is with you, who or what can come against you?

Believe in the promises of the Lord.

Believe that He is your Abba Father.

Believe that where you walk, the ground trembles because you bring the Spirit of the living God with you everywhere your feet tread.

You have to truly believe that wherever you walk, the air shifts, the stress releases, the hatred is nullified, and that which was meant for bad will turn out for good.

The Mask

I was living a happy life until I was diagnosed with Stage 3 Throat Cancer. Within a month, my life had turned upside down. As an entrepreneur, I would go to networking meetings, social events, and meetings. As a believer, I would go to many churches and consult/coach with many ministry leaders and believers. But when I got diagnosed and the pain became unbearable and then I was forced to start my treatments, my life changed.

My treatment consisted of seven weeks of radiation therapy five days a week, Monday through Friday. I also had to undergo chemotherapy treatment once a week for seven weeks. The actual act of chemotherapy was a breeze. I would sit in a comfortable recliner and they would intravenously inject different types of fluids into my body. The radiation treatment was a nightmare.

The radiation treatment I had to take required a high level of precision and timing. They would lay me down on a futuristic-looking cot, which was attached to a massive machine that would circle around my head. It took the doctor and specialized software about a week to line up the machine precisely to aim a laser that would only target the affected areas of my throat. Being that there was no room for error they had to make sure that I wouldn't move under any circumstance, not even for a cough or sneeze.

If the laser was off, it could mean trouble for my vocal cords and my ability to swallow for the rest of my life.

I was challenged every single day to get under a mask and to be strapped onto a table for 35 days.

So, to make sure that I couldn't move at all once the treatment started, they put a plastic covering over my face and shoulders and heated it up. Once it got hot, it molded itself to my face, neck, and shoulder. As the plastic stretched, little holes appeared inside it. The only big holes in the mask were around my eyes and mouth. Basically, they had created a mask that had been molded to exactly fit my face.

When it came time for my treatments, I would lie on the cot, and they would fit the mask over my face, neck, and shoulders. The scary part was that they would then strap the mask down onto the cot so that I would be unable to move from my upper shoulders to the top of my head.

In the beginning, it was all well and good. The first few treatments were a breeze. However, I quickly sensed something growing inside of me at an alarming rate. It was an acute illustration of claustrophobia – an extreme or irrational fear of confined places. I didn't hide it from my family, but the overwhelming words of encouragement and support stopped me from mentioning it again. However, internally I knew I was in trouble.

I had to go to radiation treatment five days a week, Monday through Friday. Before the end of the first week, even with all the support and prayers I knew that people were offering up on my behalf, I felt in my heart I wouldn't be able to finish the planned schedule. The mental anguish of being strapped onto the table was rapidly becoming too much for me to bear. I would think about it throughout the day. It would keep me up at night, knowing that the next morning I would be strapped onto that table under that horrific mask.

My doctor did prescribe some anti-anxiety medication for me. By the end of the second week, I was taking them, relying on them. As the treatment went on, my throat got sore, then very sore, then incredibly sore. Every time I swallowed, I experienced a level-9 pain. To make matters worse, due to the chemotherapy, I started vomiting non-stop for two or three days a week.

My fear became too real. Five days a week, I was going to be strapped under the mask, the technicians were going to leave the room, the radiation machine would circle around my head, making a loud, humming noise, and then I was going to throw up! No one was going to know and I was going to either die or have a traumatic time under that mask until they rushed in and freed me from it, only to make me repeat it because I had to complete the full treatment every day.

I tried to fight against myself to not think about it – to little avail. I have always been a big believer in the power of the spoken word, so I was reluctant to express to anyone the fear I was going through. It got to the point, though, that I couldn't help it. I expressed to my wife that I didn't want to go. The fear was real and I didn't want to face it anymore. It got to the point where I would make us late to my appointments every day. Maybe I was hoping they would drop me as a patient, I don't know. Either way, it didn't work. They took me into the radiation room every time I showed up, regardless of how late I got there.

I began taking the anti-anxiety pills as soon as I got them. I was supposed to take one at a time, which I did, but then I started taking two at a time and, sometimes I would take three!

My wife, Maria, had been a rock during the entire process. When I was weak, which was more than I ever thought I would be, she was strong. She would pray over me, speak life into my situations, declare peace in my mind, and make sure I was well taken care of.

She started to ask me about the pills, realizing that I had become overly dependent on them in order to make it through my radiation treatments. She did her best to convince me that I didn't need them. That it was all in my head. That I was strong. I was a leader, and I was too smart to be deceived into believing I needed those pills. She promised that she would sit there with the technicians outside the room and make sure I was all right. Nothing changed, though. I kept taking the pills... I had to.

"Honey, you're a man of faith. You don't need to depend on those pills."

"Babe, claustrophobia is a real thing and every time I go there, I am literally being strapped down to a table and being left alone in a closed room. My battle is mental and the pills help me deal with it. I'm not fighting a spiritual fight here. I need these pills if I'm going to finish my treatment. It has nothing to do with my belief in God," I answered.

"Just remember," she answered back. "God is with you and if God is with you, who or what can be against you? The same way He will help you fight cancer he can help you with claustrophobia."

When she told me that, that's when I thought – *but what if God isn't with me?*

I took three pills that day and went to the treatment. That night I prayed and asked God to be with me in my next treatment. I prayed, "Lord if you come with me, I won't take any pills. I need to

"We'll do it, us two, just you and me."

know, though, that you are coming with me. We'll do it, us two, just you and me." It was one of the scariest prayers I had ever offered up.

It's amazing how often it happens, once you decide to put your full trust in God, that something happens to make matters worse. That morning I woke up nauseated, which was my biggest fear of being strapped under the mask. *What if I throw up while I'm strapped in the mask? There is no one else in the room and the radiation machine is loud. How would they know I'm not choking on my own spit or vomit?*

I grabbed the bottle and took out two anti-anxiety pills, thinking I was exercising my faith because I wasn't going to take three. Mind you, I couldn't swallow anything, I had to crush my pills in a blue pill crusher. I would crush the pills into dust and mix it with water and put it through the feeding tube that protruded through my stomach.

(A feeding tube is exactly that, it's a rubber tube that they surgically attach to the top of your stomach. The way you 'eat' is they give you a large syringe-looking device that you connect to the tube. Then, you pour whatever liquid into the feeding tube and it goes directly to your stomach.)

As I put two pills into the pill crusher and shut the lid, I realized that the color of blue was familiar to me. I couldn't stop thinking how I knew that shade of blue. Sort of like how, at times, I'll see an actor and would wrack my brain to figure out how I know him or her. The thought wouldn't leave me until I'd Google the actor and see their history, so I could remember where I knew him or her.

Those that know me know I'm a big sports fan and blue is an important color for me. When I had the logo of my company created, I made sure I used the Dallas Cowboys blue. I'm also an avid college basketball fan and a fan of the Duke Blue Devils. They also have a particular shade of blue in their uniforms. As a Duke fan, I root against the North Carolina Tar Heels. They use a baby blue color. I make sure to never buy any clothes or put anything in my home that's baby blue. So, I might be more familiar with the color blue than probably most people except for painters. But on this particular day, I found it odd for me to focus on how the shade of blue of my pill crusher was familiar to me. I concentrated on it, like a dog on a bone not wanting to let it go. *Why is this color so familiar?*

Once I crushed the pills and went to pour the dust into a vial, I remembered shopping at the mall and seeing a shiny blue rock that I felt could help my young sister-in-law. She was scared of things that I felt she didn't need to be scared of. The pill crusher was the same color of blue as the courage rock I had bought Rebecca!

I experienced an epiphany regarding the pill crusher. It wasn't simply breaking apart the pills I consumed, the pill crusher became my source of strength. It became where I ran to in times of trouble. It became my strong fortress in the storm. However, what I realized was that, just as the blue stone was never meant to be the source of courage for my sister in law, meaning that she was never meant to trust in the stone itself. In like manner, my epiphany was that I was never meant to trust in the pills or the blue pill crusher. The same way my sister-in-law had the courage stored up inside of her all along, I had my faith stored up inside of me.

I had taken the pills ever since they were prescribed to me. But that day… that was a different day. A day that carried within it a defining moment in my treatment and my faith.

Lord, I need You right now. You know how scared I am. You know that I've been dependent on the chemicals of the pills to dull my senses enough so that I can sleepwalk through the treatment. I don't want to sleepwalk anymore. I don't want to rely on anything but You. Instill the confidence I need to go to my appointment today without the use of the pills. I thank You in advance for the work You are going to do in me

I don't want to sleepwalk anymore.

today. In your name Jesus, the name above all names, I pray. Amen.

I put the blue pill crusher down and shortly thereafter walked out of the house alongside my wife. At that point in time, I wasn't able to speak at all, I had to write down what I wanted to communicate in a pad with a pen. When my wife asked me if I had taken the pills, I just shook my head no. I had left the pad and pen and couldn't communicate to her that I wasn't going to take the pills anymore.

I was weak. I was scared. I was nervous, and I could barely communicate. I managed to squeak out, "How can I testify about trusting in God when this is over if I don't put my trust in Him?"

She put the car in reverse, and as we started to move, she patted me twice on the left knee and said, "Good boy. You never needed them." We drove off, she humming a tune and me praying with all my might in my head, consciously aware of the fear that tried to invade my being the closer we got to the doctor's office.

That day, I fought a familiar foe, a foe I had known all my life. I fought against myself, against my own self-doubt, and a debilitating fear that had led me to believe I couldn't get my radiation treatment without the help of pills. When I realized that the color of the pill crusher was the same color as the courage rock I had bought my sister-in-law, something shifted in my mindset. Before, I thought I needed the pills. However, at that very moment, I knew I didn't. There's a difference when you think you know something compared to when you know you know something.

I took in a few deep breaths before laying down on the cot as the technicians waited, one holding the dreaded mask. *Lord, in your name,* I prayed in my mind and I laid myself down. About a minute later, I was strapped onto the table, fully aware and conscious, and the technicians left me alone. They turned on the loud machine and it began to circle around me and do what it was made to do. As I thought about that, I too, felt I was doing what I was made to do. I was made to believe and to trust in God.

I expected to fight waves of panic and anxiety. I expected to be more scared than ever. I expected to tough it out, being that I was already strapped to the table. I expected to regret not using the anti-anxiety pills. My expectations were never met. I laid there in peace, softly humming along to a song my brothers and I used to sing many years ago. I came to the conclusion that, indeed, God had been with me every single time I was afraid to be strapped under the mask. Bringing my faith with me instead of taking the pills made all the difference in the world. It was the easiest time I had spent during a treatment.

I realized God wasn't with me based on my actions. God wasn't with me everywhere I went because I deserved it. The Almighty was with me because He said He would be. God was with me because He's neither a man nor a son of man to lie. I realized the truth of that verse. God was with me everywhere I went, and even though I would never be perfect or one hundred percent holy, I couldn't get in His way of raising a banner and fighting for me.

DECLARE & BELIEVE THIS
God isn't with me because I deserve it... **He's with me because He said He would!**

I never took another anti-anxiety pill after that day. Was I still scared? Yes. Was I suddenly cured or liberated from thoughts of claustrophobia? No. But my mindset had shifted. I believed in the verse that says, "If God is with you, who or what can come against you?"

The Fierce Urgency of Now

If you could ever really believe that verse in your spirit, it can make all the difference in the world for you, for the rest of your life.

Chapter 10

Provision

Unpredictability

If there is one truth about this life on earth, it can be this: it's unpredictable. On any given day, something can happen and alter the trajectory of your life. Teams that are supposed to win don't always win. Friends that have always been trustworthy will, at times, betray you. A sudden accident involving other people can turn your fifteen-minute commute to work to forty-five minutes. A fall on a slippery surface can break your arm. Pipes bursting in your home can suddenly cost you thousands of dollars. A phone call from your daughter can change your status from father or mother to grandfather or grandmother.

Life is unpredictable, even for those people who live their lives by schedules, finishing task lists, and regimenting their lives as if they were in the military. At times, you will feel as if you're in a season of abundance, but without warning, you may find yourself in the position of needing to ask for help.

The problem is that we aren't seers; we can't see the future. We don't know what we're going to need in five or twenty-five years. There is no silver bullet, no magic pill, no secret sauce to drink that will prepare us for what we might need in the future. However, in the Bible, God often talks about having provision for us. (Provision, in the context in which I'm using it, means to have what you need in a future time when you will need it.) There are many verses, many promises, regarding us having God-given provision.

2 Corinthians 9:8

"And God is able to bless you abundantly, so that in all things at all times, having all that you need, you will abound in every good work."

John 10:10

"The thief comes only to steal and kill and destroy; I have come that they may have life, and have it to the full."

Luke 12:7

"Indeed, the very hairs of your hair are all numbered. Don't be afraid; you are worth more than many sparrows."

Luke 12:24

"Consider the ravens: They do not sow or reap, they have no storeroom or barn, yet God feeds them. And how much more valuable you are than birds!"

It takes faith to believe that, no matter what happens in your life, God will have preordained provision or people into place long before to help you. While what happened to you may have surprised you and suddenly thrust a time of need upon you, it didn't surprise God. In order to believe that, you need to believe that God is omnipotent and the Alpha and Omega, and that He knows everything that is going to or can happen to your life.

Teenage Pregnancy

I remember vividly the day I found out my teenage daughter was pregnant. It wasn't a phone call; it was a sudden bout of vomit that my teenage daughter, Mia, couldn't hold back after having breakfast one morning. It occurred during the summer when my three children were visiting from Rhode Island. Mia, being the eldest, was a teenager and the one with whom I would have the most conversation with. We were, and are, extremely close. When I found out she was pregnant, I had so many emotions go through me, I didn't know how to handle it. I lamented:

She ruined her life!

What about her future?

This is my fault.

I should have been able to prevent this!

I went for a drive, not sure of where I was going. I just needed some fresh air and time to think things through. I didn't want to say anything to my daughter that either us of would regret later. About an hour later, I found myself in my pastor's office. Full disclosure, my pastor at the time was my brother-in-law, Pastor Joe. I had been attending his church because my wife, his sister, was attending his church when we met. Although I loved the people and the sermons, there were times when I felt that I was at the wrong church.

I speak, read, write, and comprehend much better in English than I do in Spanish. Pastor Joe leads an all-Spanish church. Not only was it an all-Spanish-speaking, but it was made up of people from different parts of Latin and Central America, beautiful people, every single one of them. For those of you who don't know, the Spanish spoken in different parts of the world are different. The Spanish I know and speak, as an American-born citizen from Puerto Rican parents, is not the best Spanish. I would have preferred to go to a church where people wouldn't laugh at what I said, even though they laughed at me with love, not malice. We even attended a very popular English church in the Tampa area for about six months. But for a reason I wouldn't realize till much later, there we were, back at this all-Spanish-speaking church.

Pastor Joe, I believe had some official training in therapy/counseling and in de-escalating tense situations. If he hadn't, he's a gifted natural and could make a living teaching it if he wanted to.

My point is this, God knew Mia would get pregnant and it would cause me grief, sadness, and feelings of guilt. God had me at that church because the language of the services wouldn't matter when I would need the right person at the right time. By the way, Pastor Joe speaks better English than I do. God knew that I would come to need a pastor who was empathetic, and who would not judge me for how I spoke and carried on as he listened to me and let me speak and cry out my fears and emotions before he went to work on putting me back together again. Growing up in church, I had seen people condemned for how they behaved during a severe crisis. I didn't need a pastor like that. I wasn't acting very Christian-like.

By the time I got back home, I, who had left with grief and shame, came back with hope and love to offer to my daughter and my coming grandchild. I believe that my time with him salvaged my relationship with my daughter. I believe whole-heartedly that Pastor Joe was who I needed as a spiritual covering during that time. I believe that God had ordained for me to go to his office on that fateful day. God had, as His Word says, set provision for me before I got the point of crisis.

Recipes

As a ghostwriter, I have had the privilege of writing many books for many people. There were two books I had the pleasure of working on that are important to the point I want to make in this chapter. Both books are about clean living through proper eating. I helped write two incredible books that have done very well in the market and for their respective authors on plant-based recipes and foods that help your body heal from any sicknesses or diseases.

Fast-forward to the time I was diagnosed with cancer. Once God got me through cancer, I had to find a whole new way to eat. I was mentally preparing myself for the daunting task of searching all over the Internet to find the best foods for me to eat. Then I remembered that, in my laptop, I just happened to have the top recipes of two very credible professionals on what to eat and on what not to eat. I'd had those in my laptop *prior* to being diagnosed!

What I'm saying is that God knew I would need that information. He knew my recovery and immunity from getting cancer again would depend on my diet. So, prior to me being diagnosed, He placed those two experts in my path so that when the time came when I needed their expertise, I would not have to ask for it – because I would already have it!

> **DECLARE & BELIEVE THIS**
>
> **I don't always have to pray for it...**
> **God has already provided it!**

As a child of God, you have to believe that you will not be put in a situation where you are not, in some way, equipped to deal with it. Think of all the times you've cried or felt that there was no way out of whatever dire situation you'd found yourself in. Somehow, some way, God brought you through. If you look closer, you might see that He had preset things or people in your life that were already at your disposal before the calamity befell you.

Sign Language

When I was eight years old, my oldest sister, Marylyn, befriended a girl who was deaf. She was the only "outsider" I recall coming to our house enough times that I would remember her when I was older. I don't remember exactly when it happened, because I would imagine it took many times for it to happen, but during that time, I learned how to sign the alphabet using American Sign Language. I don't think I was the only one. I believe most of my siblings learned it too, as we were a welcoming group and wanted to communicate with the friendly girl who would come to visit.

More than seventy years before my diagnosis, in the small town called San Tursè, Puerto Rico, Eugenio Lugo, a then eight-month old child had a bout with Scarlet Fever that left him deaf. He never heard or spoke after that. When he was seventeen, he moved to Brooklyn, New York, where he met and married his wife. When I was eight years old, learning how to sign the alphabet in Rochester, New York, there was a little girl of six years old in Brooklyn who was starting to learn how to sign in order to communicate with her father.

During my treatment, my throat had just about closed itself off. Swallowing was extremely difficult and speaking was impossible. I couldn't utter a word — my voice was totally gone. That was the lowest moment of my ordeal with cancer. I was losing weight quickly, I was vomiting non-stop every day, I was suffering with anxiety to go to my radiation treatment, and the worst part was, I couldn't talk. I couldn't express to anyone what I needed, whether for comfort or necessity. I couldn't tell anyone how worried I was. I had no way of verbally communicating with anyone.

But God knew I would be in that situation. That's why, when I was eight years old, He brought a young girl to my house to teach me sign language. At that same time, there was a six-year-old girl in Brooklyn learning how to sign.

That little girl who learned sign language at six years old to communicate with her father, became my wife many years later. When I was weak, when I felt beaten, when I couldn't talk, when I was at the lowest point of my life, I would look at my wife and move my fingers and she would understand everything I needed to convey.

God, the Alpha, and Omega of my life knew that, when I would turn fifty, I would need a way out of a no-way-out situation. He designed it so what I'd learned as a fun game when I was a kid turned out to be my only means of communication when I would be so weak I couldn't pick up a pen to write.

I believe you are reading this because you need to understand in your mind and spirit that, if you are in a tough situation, it may have surprised you, but it did not surprise your God. Take a look around you, what you have around you, who you have become, and who you have around you. Surely, there is no need to despair. God has a habit of making a way when there seems to be no way.

God knew I would need to marry someone who knew sign language. He knew I would not have the time, when I was sick, to teach my primary caregiver how to sign. So God taught Maria at an early age how to understand the art of sign language so that when I, His son, whom He cares for regardless of how unworthy I am, would be at my lowest moment, He would show me once again that He had already set in place a provision to get me through dark times.

During the worst times of my life physically, standing alongside me with a wedding ring I had gifted to her was a godly woman, fully equipped, not only to help me spiritually, but also equipped to provide the provision I would need from a seemingly no-win situation.

I'm not special. I'm not holy. I am undeserving of God's mercy and grace. I think that you're much like me; at the end of the day, a flawed person who tries to please God in the midst of a fallen and unbelieving world. Thankfully, His mercy and grace doesn't depend on us. He gives it liberally and freely.

When Moses was stuck between the sea and the pharaoh's army, he had a staff already in his hand. When the Philistines came to attack Samson, he found a dry donkey's jawbone, just waiting to be picked up and utilized. When David fought against Goliath, he found five smooth stones right before the battle, just lying around.

When I needed to change my diet because of cancer, I had already written books on how to eat clean. When I needed wise counsel, although I had not been attending the church I wanted to, I was helped by a pastor who was fully equipped, knowing how to handle my situation. When I was at my lowest and weakest moment and could only use my fingers, I could communicate with my wife through sign language.

I am a believer through experience and testimony that God will preset provision for you. When the storms come, and they will, you'll find a safe port to ride it out. You just have to look around for it.

Yes, life is unpredictable for us. Yes, in life we will suffer. Yes, in life we will have moments of fear, uncertainty, doubt, sickness, and even moments of unbelief. But none of that, while allowed to happen to us, is meant to kill us. In fact, it's meant to strengthen us. But it can't if we don't see beyond the circumstances.

Fear not, God has preset provision for you to get you through every challenging moment. Not only to get you through it, but also to strengthen you so that you don't worry as much the next time.

Chapter 11

Bones of Praise

Dried Bones

There's a story in the Bible I've heard many times. I've even preached on it on several occasions. It depicts one of God's greatest victories in the Old Testament. It's found in Judges 15, verses 14–17.

[14] And when he came unto Lehi, the Philistines shouted against him: and the Spirit of the Lord came mightily upon him, and the cords that were upon his arms became as flax that was burnt with fire, and his bands loosed from off his hands.

[15] And he found a new jawbone of an ass, and put forth his hand, and took it, and slew a thousand men therewith.

[16] And Samson said, With the jawbone of an ass, heaps upon heaps, with the jaw of an ass have I slain a thousand men.

[17] And it came to pass, when he had made an end of speaking, that he cast away the jawbone out of his hand, and called that place Ramathlehi.

Do you remember the story? It's an amazing thing that a man without modern weapons of the time that a man could defeat 1,000 armed soldiers with something like a jawbone of a donkey.

Equally amazing are the teachings we can find in these few, short verses. I'm going to share my thoughts on two of them.

The first thing that amazes me is how there was a jawbone just lying around. The Bible speaks to us often about bones. One of the most famous exchanges regarding bones is when God asked Ezekiel, "Those bones, will they live again?"

Ezekiel answered, "You are God and only you know."

I present to you that God knew Samson was going to need a weapon on that very day. So, years before, He had the donkey die there. The donkey's body decomposed until only the jawbone remained. Many years later, Samson was frantically looking for a way to defend himself and what did he find? *Provision.* He found something to aid him in a time of need. When Samson picked up that dried and dead jawbone, God gave it a new purpose. Those bones lived again!

I'm here to tell somebody reading this that, at one time you may have had an idea, a calling, a purpose, but for whatever reasons, it had withered and died. Maybe it's because you don't feel that close to God that it has died. Maybe it's because you did nothing to maximize your potential and it has

What you thought was dead, God is about to repurpose in your life.

died. Maybe you never thought you would be able to do it and you ignored it, starving it to death. But you need to know that what you might have thought was dead, what you might have thought had gotten past your grip, God is about to repurpose it in your life. Oh, if only you would come to an agreement with me on that! What you thought was dead, God is about to repurpose in your life.

Maybe you're stuck in a rut in your marriage and it has never been what you have dreamed it to be. Your ideal marriage can come to life. Maybe you're not living the life you wanted to live. Your dream life can come to life. Maybe your relationship with family members has gotten sour. That, too, can be resurrected. The donkey's owner figured that since it was dead, it was useless. It wasn't useless. It was waiting to be repurposed.

In order to know most stories, it's important to know the backstory. Here's the backstory on what happened prior to Samson picking up the jawbone.

When You Surrender to Praise

Here's the second thing: Samson was hiding out in Judah. *Judah means praise*. When his enemies came in force to get him, they spoke to the leaders of Judah. The leaders of Judah spoke to Samson. Samson surrendered himself to the children of Judah. They tied him up and led him to his enemies. It was then that they attacked and Samson found the jawbone and killed a thousand of them.

What I'm telling you is this. Like Samson surrendered to the tribe of Judah, which means praise, in order to win your battles, you need to surrender first to praise. When you understand the power of praise, you uncover a paradigm shift.

Praising is not asking. Praising is not begging. Praising is not throwing yourself onto the floor at someone's mercy. Praising is giving thanks for what will happen in your life, regardless of how bleak the present situation may look. Praising is lifting up a joyous sound in advance of the miracle that God is going to perform on your situation. Praising is believing in a good ending while you're still at the beginning of a trial. In order to praise like that, you have to believe in your inner core that God is the Alpha and Omega and knows every moment of your life.

When you unleash your praise ahead of knowing the outcome, jawbones are found. A way out is revealed. Help comes from places you never thought it would.

I'm here to remind you that you have a jawbone of your own. There are things in your life that you used to do, sins you used to commit, that came naturally to you. However, during your walk with Christ, as your faith has grown, those things you used to do have become dead to you. You are no longer a drunk. You are no longer a pothead. You no longer intimidate. You no longer cheat. You no longer steal. You no longer talk the way you used to talk. You no longer treat the opposite sex the way you used to.

Those things that you used to do are now long dead. Those actions and thoughts are now a part of your testimony. I'd like you to prepare yourself for the next time the enemy attacks. The next time the enemy accuses you, I want you to pick up those dead bones in your life. The dead bones God has given you to fight with are now your personal testimony. Look at what God has done in you. Sure, you may not be perfect, but you're not the same as you used to be. There are things you used to do that you've died to, for the sake of living for Christ. Those things that you've killed from your life in your pursuit of Jesus are your jawbones. Give God praise and allow the Spirit of the Lord to come upon you. Pick up that jawbone and repel the enemy's attacks. You are not ill-equipped for battle, you carry dead jawbones inside of you.

The problem is that some people still don't realize who they are in Christ. Instead of judging themselves by being washed by the blood of the Lamb and worthy of heaven, they judge themselves by their mistakes. God doesn't see you by your mistakes, He sees you through a lens that's filtered through the blood of Jesus. He doesn't see you as a sinner. He sees you as His beautiful bride.

When I was diagnosed with cancer, I thanked God. People who don't know God would probably think me foolish, confused, or maybe flat-out dumb. But after the shock wore off, I knew He would get me through it. I knew I was going to go through a process, but I also knew the process was not meant to kill me, but to strengthen me. So I thanked him. I surrendered myself to my praise.

My voice, still strong at the time, filled my house singing and recounting His glory as I gave him praise. I praised him for the life I had already lived. I praised Him for my family. I praised Him for all He had brought me through. And I praised Him because He was going to get me through cancer. And... He did.

PART THREE
Time Waits for No One

"The bad news is, time flies...
The good news is, you're the pilot!"

Michael Altshuler, Author

"The bad news is, time flies...

The good news is, God's your pilot!"

Brian Zaas *(My Life Coach)*

Chapter 12

The In-Between Time

Perhaps God has you reading this because, while He knows the purpose He has for your life, you may have gotten yourself stuck. Possibly, your way of thinking needs readjusting or your actions need realigning. I call this a paradigm shift. *A paradigm means examples, standards, theories, ideas, patterns, and models.*

For someone to experience a paradigm shift, the change has to go all the way to the person's core. It has to be something so ingrained in the person that it cannot just affect how someone responds to questions or stimuli. A paradigm shift alters your fundamental view of everything around you. As a result, it changes how you react to things. It also clarifies for you your non-negotiable traits, the things you will not surrender at any cost.

I think God may have put this book in your hand to prepare you. A paradigm shift is starting to befall you. You're going to start to look at the world a little differently. You're going to start looking at your time on earth with more scrutiny. You're going to examine the gifts and talents you have and gauge them with serious intentions.

Many of God's children are in need of a paradigm shift. We have found a way to meld our belief in God with the comforts of conforming to this fallen world. The thing about paradigm shifts is that they don't happen instantaneously. You don't just hear a quote that speaks to you and it changes your perception about your entire life. There's a period of time that denotes the person you were and the person you are called to be. I call that time, the in-between time.

The In-Between Time

The in-between time is a period in a person's life that contrasts where a person is with what the person becomes. For example, you may be saved and attending your church faithfully. However, God's calling in your life might be to become a teacher, a preacher, or a pastor. The in-between time is the time between you answering the call of salvation to when you live up to your God-given destiny.

The in-between time is dangerous. At times, it can be compared to the valley. You can have all the gifts in the world for something specific, but for whatever reason, you still haven't achieved that status. For example, you could be the best guitarist in your church, but you're not playing your guitar with the worship team, even though you want to. You may be the best actress in your church, but you didn't get the lead role in the Christmas play. You might be the best speaker in your church, but you didn't get invited to give a talk at the men's retreat.

The main reason why you aren't being asked to do what you're very good at could be that God doesn't trust you with His name yet. When you are elevated through position or title in the body of Christ, whether we like it or not, a certain responsibility to protect and defend God's laws is thrust upon us. People look at us and expect us to be different than them. They expect our marriages to be perfect. They expect us to be good stewards of our finances. They expect us to be model fathers. Sure, that has nothing to do with the gift God has given you, but believe me when I tell you, it comes with the job.

When I started attending my brother-in-law's church, I got antsy. There were very few leaders there and even fewer people who were willing to take on a leadership role. I grew up in church and in ministry and I could fake being a perfect Christian as well as anyone. The truth was that I had just met my wife and I had just come to know the Lord again. I still had many bad habits from my fourteen years of backsliding and acting a fool. However, I saw the need at the church, so I got antsy to help out.

I had plenty of great, in-depth conversations with my pastor on topics from the Bible to how ministers are expected to act when facing the challenges of being in leadership. Since my early twenties, I have always tried to utilize my God-given abilities to help others grow and evolve and I saw a need there. I was aware that he realized that I knew how to be a minister. I knew that he knew I was capable of either leading the youth, or helping to start up the worship team, or work with the men. I felt my pastor would soon put me into a position to really help the ministry.

However, six months passed and he hadn't tagged me in. A year passed and I was still on the sidelines. Two years passed and, even with all the glaring holes I could see that I could help fill, he hadn't called on me to help.

At first, I was antsy. I was ready to work. I couldn't wait. But as the time went on, I got upset and angry. *Why doesn't he want me to help? There are so many ways I can help this ministry!*

Internally, I was challenged with the reasons I wanted to help so badly. Did I just want some limelight? Did I just want to be out front? I'd always had leadership tendencies. When my son Isaiah started to play organized basketball, I became one of the YMCA coaches. When he moved up to play AAU, I ingrained myself into the organization and became the head coach. I had to look into myself and determine why I wanted to be in leadership so badly – especially when I wasn't living as godly a life as I should have been.

God was setting me up for a paradigm shift, but I didn't know it.

Patience, to me, means waiting and being okay with waiting.

Patience dictates the ticking of time when we are residing in the *in-between time*. If there is one thing many men, myself included, don't have much of, it's patience. We can wait for things and we can bide our time for things – but that's different than having patience. Everyone waits. Patience, to me, means waiting and being okay with waiting. Those with patience can wait and whistle with a smirk on their faces. Those without patience shift, pace, grumble, and argue while they wait.

And that's what I had been doing, complaining while I was waiting. As the time wore on, I stopped looking at all the holes I could fill and I started paying attention to what was being said from the pulpit. I stopped thinking of heading up a ministry and doing things the way we'd done them at my father's church. I started to understand the heart and doctrine of my current pastor. It got to the point that I started to go to church simply to receive what God had for me.

Once I had gone through the paradigm shift and I was totally comfortable with *not helping out* or leading a ministry, God opened the doors for me. My mother-in-law headed up the children's church. On a Sunday, one of the scheduled teachers became unavailable. On my way to church, she asked me if I could give the class that day. At first, I declined it, saying that I hadn't had time to prepare myself, but she would hear none of that.

"Just open your mouth. You're good at that," she said, with love.

I had fun with it and presented a Bible story to a group of eight to ten-year-olds. After the service, my mother-in-law asked me if I would be willing to serve, alternating with the other teacher every other Sunday.

"Would that be okay with the pastor?" I asked.

"He gave me the authority to bring in the teachers I see fit. Do it."

I became an alternate teacher to the children and that's how I started in ministry again. A year later, I was their only teacher. A year after that, I was put in charge of the youth. Soon thereafter, I was a part of the worship team and led the worship services every third week. A year after that, I was put in charge of the youth group. Two years more and I was put in charge of the men's group. A year following that, my wife and I were put in charge of the marriage ministry.

Two years later, we were attending a new church, a much larger church, and we were just regular parishioners again. God had equipped us at my brother-in-law's church. I had experienced a paradigm shift and had to come to grips for the reasons why I desired the positions I wanted. Once I came to the understanding that it's all about God, that's when God opened the doors.

The in-between time is when God shows you His glory on a personal level. Before you teach it or preach it, you have to live it. Giving your pastor good lip service is not the way to ministry. Loving the Lord and seeking His will for your life is how it's done.

Beware the in-between time, because if you don't acquire patience, it can break you. Come to terms that you aren't where you want to be and don't blame anybody for it. Thank God for giving you in-between time to better yourself, whether it's in music, sports, business, or ministry.

What a freeing feeling it is to know that you don't have the be the all-wise, all-knowing expert yet. Take advantage of the in-between time to study that thing that calls to you. Use the in-between time to ensure that you have buried your past and all the evil or hurt that it held. A championship fighter doesn't win the fight because he can fight. He wins because, prior to the fight, he maximized the time before the fight and trained wisely. He restricted his diet and didn't allow himself to indulge in foods or to participate in things that could be detrimental to his health.

One of the important things to know about the in-between time is, it's meant to be temporary. You are not meant to live your life in the in-between time. Those that have, have never lived up to their potential. They never see their dreams or God-given calling fulfilled.

Potential

Potential doesn't last forever. A young basketball player can have a ton of potential as he or she starts high school. Everyone could see that, at their age, they could go right to the very top. However, if during their high school years, they start smoking marijuana and drinking alcohol, or they start to miss practice and get in trouble with the coach, their potential can shrivel up and die. Ten years later, that kid who had so much potential but squandered it, lost any potency his potential once held. He is no longer greeted with smiles and given words of encouragement of what he could be. Instead, he's looked upon with pity.

The in-between times tests potential against personal will. Yes, you may have a calling to be a pastor, but if you'd rather go drinking beer with your friends instead of going to church and getting into God's Word, your calling will die within you.

The in-between times tests potential against personal will.

If you find yourself in an in-between time, I'm happy for you. It's a time of freedom and liberation. It's a time of preparation and learning. Once you're into your calling, it's a time for giving. Once you've started your own company, it's time to work. It's hard to build yourself up when you're constantly giving parts of yourself away. Use the in-between time to build yourself up to what you're called to do. Just make sure you don't die there.

Chapter 13

45 is 45

Time

The earth rotates around the sun constantly. It makes one 360-degree rotation relative to distant stars, in 23 hours, 56 minutes, and 04.1 seconds. The seconds tick on a stopwatch constantly. Even when the watch runs out of the battery and the seconds hand on the watch stops to move, time keeps moving.

We have all been given 24 hours that makes up our day. No one gets more, no one gets less. The richest men in the world can't buy more. The best conniver in the world can't trick anyone or anything to give them more. We get 24 hours for every day. No more. No less.

The thing about time is that you use it up, whether you mean to or not. If you lay down and take a nap for ten minutes, you've used up those ten minutes. You can't cry to God and say, "Wait. I didn't really use that time, I was taking a nap. I need that time back!"

Each of us has been allotted a certain amount of time on this earth. God has granted blessings for people with long life and God has decreed that some people only live a cherished few years – or even months – on this planet. The biggest factor in becoming who you will become in your life is how you spend your time. Some people may have advantages from family lineage but even with "knowing

The biggest factor in becoming who you will become in your life is how you spend your time.

the right people," if you don't spend the time becoming good at something, you will not become good at that thing.

45 is 45

Too many of God's children are stuck in a rut. Let's forget about attacks, issues, spiritual warfare, illnesses, and sin for a moment. I mean that they are stuck in a rut in terms of progress. There are parts of their lives that have not moved forward for years. They were in a failing marriage five years ago and they're still in a failing marriage now. They have been battling with the behavior of their children five years ago and now those kids are teenagers or young adults and they're still battling with their behavior.

Five years ago, financially, they were sick and tired of barely making ends meet. They hated the fact that they could only go out to eat maybe only once or twice a month. They always shopped in the clearance section. They never had a choice in which car they wanted to buy; they bought whatever they could afford.

The problem is this – five years ago, maybe you were sick and tired of living in a financial rut but if we fast-forward to today, you're still living in a financial rut! Maybe you're still barely making ends meet. Maybe you still can't go out to eat as much as you'd like. Or maybe you're not that bad off financially, but you hate your job.

The bottom line is this: there are many people that are not living the lives they'd like to live. What if I told you I have the answer to your problem? Would you allow yourself to believe it? I'm about to tell you the secret. The secret of how anyone can change their life so that they are living the life they want to live in just a few years' time.

Here it is: *Learn how to leverage the 45.*

Everybody has 45 minutes of free time per day. There is nothing that you are doing in your life that you can't take 45 minutes to dedicate to something else.

How I Became a Writer

After working for corporate America for twenty years, and at my last corporate job getting warned that our entire department might be forced to close, I realized I needed a change. I was a manager at the time and had invested much more than the expected forty hours per week. I would get to work early, stay late, talk to my team members while at home, and prepare presentations during weekends. Our team was doing well; however, I had been told that we were all about to be let go. I was ordered not to tell my team members. They were going to find out they were going to lose their jobs on the day they were laid off.

I was sick and tired of not being able to control my financial earnings. I had always been told I was a good writer. In fact, I had been working on a fantasy novel for years and had been given great feedback by those I'd allowed to read it. I loved to write, to create a story, add characters... to take words and put them onto a blank page, then create conflict and resolution that could light up someone's imagination. My written words have been responsible for making people laugh and even cry.

Right around that time, my brother-in-law, Peter, a former pastor turned publisher, decided to finally write the book that had been in his heart for years. When he was pastoring, he preached a sermon series that started a revival in his church and he wanted to convert those sermons into a book. His problem was that, although he was an amazing speaker and had great ideas of what he wanted to say in his book, writing was not his strength.

He asked me if I could help him put his book together. I told him I'd try but I was very busy at work, even though I knew I was probably not going to work there for much longer. I was still holding on to hope that something could change and we would keep our jobs.

He sent me some notes he had written and we spoke at length on the book he wanted to write. I loved the content he had. It was brilliant. His book was to be called, *Excuses, Excuses, Which One is Yours?* (You can find it at any online book retailer.) The premise of the book was that too many of us have allowed ourselves to believe the excuses we give ourselves and the excuses we give God, and because of that, we never live up to our potential. The book goes on to reveal the truth about excuses, that they're lies and that they all come from the father of lies.

As we worked on the book, I suggested that we find a Life Coach to interview on how to live an excuse-free life. I didn't want to motivate people to live an excuse-free life and then not give them the tools to be able to do so. Peter thought it was a great idea and tasked me to do it, since it was my idea. So, I interviewed a few Christian Life Coaches. It completed the book and the book became a huge success. Peter went all over the country, and even outside of the country, to share his message. He even brought with him *No Excuses* t-shirts, *No Excuses* hats, and *No Excuses* rubber bracelets.

The book was a financial windfall for Peter and it started revivals at many of the churches where he was invited.

I reached out to one of the life coaches I had interviewed for the book. We met for coffee and he let me ramble on, on how hurt I was going to be, being let go after all I had given to the company, and how I was tired of working for someone else. Brian Zaas, the life coach, had been in my shoes. He worked at corporate America for years and then went to a start-up company, which he helped grow into a nationally recognized business. He left corporate America to follow his calling as a Christian Life Coach (and later a Pastor), which basically means he left working a 9-to-5 at someone else's company to work for himself. That's exactly what I wanted to do, but I didn't know what to do or how to even start.

"Why don't you write?" he asked.

"I'm not a writer. I don't even have a college degree. After high school, I went into the Marines. I can't get a job as a writer," I answered.

During our conversation, he started to open my mind to the possibility of being a writer. The main problem I had was that I didn't even know where or how to start.

"Start where you have favor," he advised.

"What do you mean? Where do I have favor?"

"With your brother-in-law. He works for a publishing company, doesn't he? And didn't you just help him with his book? I'm sure he can vouch for you. But, Eli." He paused for emphasis. "Don't wait to get laid off, see if you can get started now."

As we continued to talk, I, the one that had just co-written a book about excuses, gave Brian every excuse in the book, telling him why I couldn't make a living as a writer. Yes, I had written a book, but I had never read a book on how to write a book. I faked it! I wrote it the way I thought it should have been written and not how experts write books. Again, this was before we would know the success this book brought about.

"The truth is Brian, I don't have the time. My job is demanding more from me than ever. I don't have the time to start writing on the side."

Brian looked at me and then said something that changed my life forever. "Eli, if you let me, I'd like to be your life coach. I won't charge you a dime. My calling is to help navigate situations like this for God's people. What do you say?"

I was taken aback. I didn't know what life coaching would mean. I mean, I didn't want this guy I barely knew to get all up in my business. Plus, I felt weird letting him do this for me and not bless him financially. He insisted that it wouldn't get weird and that he felt led by God to walk alongside me during that season. I relented, and just like that, I had a Life Coach.

The first thing he had me do completely changed my life. He emailed me an Excel spreadsheet. The sheet was preset with time slots on the left-hand side and the days of the week on the top.

"What are the three or four most important things in your life?" he asked me.

"Uhhhh, God, family, church, and I guess my job," I answered.

I filled out the spreadsheet the following week. It was designed so that I could fill in what I did every half-hour. I filled it all in and emailed it back to him after the week was out. When we met, he confronted me.

"Why did you lie to me?" he asked.

It took all of two seconds for me to get uncomfortable.

"You said the four most important things in your life were God, family, church, and your job? But, based on your actions, there is no way that's the case."

He handed me a print-out of the spreadsheet I'd filled out. As I looked it over, he said, "Eli, you don't have any devotion time set aside for God. You don't have any time set aside for your children. Going by this, playing basketball or volleyball is more important to you than anything else you mentioned. Watching television, sometimes for four or five hours a day is also more important."

What he said to me rocked me to my core. The spreadsheet showed a typical week of my life and he was one-hundred percent correct. If someone saw how I really lived my life, they would not believe that what was most important to me was what I'd said it was. I had said God was the most important thing in my life, but when I saw the manifestations of my actions, I realized I didn't set aside any time to be with God, except for church. On days there was no church, there was no connection from my end reaching out to God. I had no time set aside for prayer and no time set aside to read His Word.

"The biggest lie you told me was that you had no time to start to make a living as a writer."

Brian had me fill out another spreadsheet that day. "I want you to write out for me your ideal life. Fill in each half-hour of the life you want to live. Once we know the destination, I can help you get there."

That meeting changed my life. From that point on, I became very conscious of how I spent my time and whom I spent it with. From that day on, I started trying to follow the ideal life I had written down. One of the big changes was in the mornings. Before, I would have coffee and get ready for work. In the *Ideal Week*, I coined a new phrase, it was now: *Coffee with Jesus.* Meaning, every morning when I drank my coffee, I would pray. I would spend time in devotion with God.

Brian also helped me to see that I had plenty of time after I got off work to learn how to become a professional writer. The guy that co-wrote the book *Excuses, Excuses*, had no excuse on why he couldn't live his dream life.

Instead of binge-watching on Netflix or watching hours upon hours of television programming, I would go to a Barnes & Noble store and read books on how to write a book. I learned, from different masters, how to construct a narrative concisely and effectively. I learned how books should start, depending on the genre. I learned about how many words should be in a book, depending on the genre. I learned the art of storytelling through the written word. I learned how to incorporate scenery and when to focus more on dialogue. My television time got swapped out for time that would help me live my dream life.

I called my brother-in-law and asked him if he thought I could be a freelance writer for his company. He happened to work for the largest Christian self-publishing company in the world! You had to jump through hoops and have a big resume to become one of their vetted writers. But Pete became my champion. He was their top publisher, and as such, his words carried weight. He got me a coveted interview with the managing editor. The stage was set for my life to change.

I have always done well with interviews but I was really nervous for that one. When I got there, I was led to a small conference room to wait for the managing editor. She entered the room carrying a manila folder and greeted me as a friend, not as an interviewer. After the usual small talk, she opened up the folder and looked at the pages inside of it, as if impressed by what she saw.

"So, Peter told me you wrote this?" she asked.

I didn't want to come off as conceited and I didn't know the protocol of how to act when you work as a ghostwriter, which was a term I was just learning about. "Well, it's Peter's words and Peter's thoughts. I just put them down on paper."

She flipped a couple of pages and proceeded to read an entire paragraph from chapter 2.

"You wrote that."

"I did," I answered, hoping that she was enjoying what she read.

She began to ask me my thought process on why I wrote certain things the way I did. I had a hard time coming up with what I thought were good answers. The truth was that I wrote the book the way I felt like it should have been written. There was no methodology I'd followed and no rhyme or reason. The content Pete gave me was so good and so full of *rhema*, it was easy to write. Besides, I had heard Peter preach hundreds of times. Capturing his voice was as easy to me as capturing mine.

"Eli, I think we can definitely use your talents here at this company. There are some books that we get from some high-profile pastors and, well, we only have one writer who can write at their level."

I didn't know what to say. So, all I said was, "Really?"

"There are definitely some things about constructing a book, pacing, and other things you're going to have to learn… but for this style of book, and we get many of these, you're already writing like a pro."

I left there as a freelance writer for one of the largest Christian publishing companies in the world. It didn't pay anything remotely close to what I was making in corporate America, but I was thrilled.

That's when I doubled down. I started by devoting at least forty-five minutes every day to learning more about how the experts wrote books. Some days it would only be fifteen minutes and other days it was two hours. The commitment I made to spend at least forty-five minutes a day uprooted my routine, as this soon became one of the top priorities of my day.

I would read blogs, look up videos on YouTube to see how others constructed books, created narrative, generated suspense, and wrote believable dialogue. Soon after, I began to invest even more of my free time learning the art of writing. I would go to a local bookstore, grab a coffee, and get three or four best sellers in front of me and, among other things, learn the tactics the authors used to start and end their books. There were so many principles, methodologies, and so many thoughts that seemed more like suggestions instead of rules, but I soaked it all in as best I could.

I traded my basketball night for a writer's critique group. Every other Tuesday evening, I got together with other wanna-be authors and writers and we would read our work to one another and have it critiqued. It was like a master class for my work to be critiqued by so many intelligent thinkers, and it was free! (To this day, even after writing more than eighty books, including some best sellers, I still go to my writer's critique group periodically. I've learned that masters become masters when they realize they always need to be students.)

About a month later, I got laid off from my job. I was at a crossroads. I loved to write, but it was barely bringing in any money. My wife was a stay-at-home wife. She had never had any children and we had recently had a daughter. She wanted to spend every possible moment with her and I didn't blame her. The problem was, as a freelance writer for that publishing company, I would not earn enough.

I wanted to give writing a go, try it hard for three to six months and see what I could do, but it was not the right move financially. Then, she rocked my world.

"Babe, I don't think you should go back to work for someone else. God's given you a gift to write. Besides, you want to be a writer. And I want you to be happy."

"No, that's okay," I answered. "I can get another good paying job and write on the side. It's important for you to spend these years with Trinity."

She looked at me, the way she normally does when she's about to tell me to do something. "Work on becoming a writer. I'll get a part-time job. Everything will work itself out. I know it."

I never looked for another job after that day. Maria got a part-time job at the sheriff's office and I became a full-time writer. The rest, as they say, is history.

Your 45

I want to challenge you to look clearly at how you are spending your time. Maybe you're living the way I was, thinking you put God first when, in fact, you barely talk to him. Maybe you've been fooling yourself into thinking that you are too busy to start something new. Maybe, just maybe, you're not living the life you desire and even worse, you're not doing anything about it.

Whatever it is you want to do with your life, go for it, so long as it's not totally unreasonable, for instance, if you're forty-eight years old and you want to be a surgeon and you only have a high-school diploma, go for something realistically attainable. But if there is something that consumes your time and you're naturally good at it, you can find forty-five minutes a day to become an expert at it.

You can find forty-five minutes a day to take an online course and get certified at something you love to do. If you want to become a guitar player but never played, you can find forty-five minutes a day to practice. You can take lessons, either in person or online. If you devote yourself to it, and if you have a natural tendency to pick it up, in five years you could become one heck of a guitar player.

Maybe this is why you're reading this book. Maybe you need to be told that you've been lying to yourself when you tell yourself that

you're too busy to follow your dreams. We all have 24 hours a day. Empires have been built on the same amount of time you have. There must be at least thousands of success stories of people who

Maybe you need to be told that you've been lying to yourself when you tell yourself that you're too busy to follow your dreams.

came from nothing and made something of themselves in ministry or business.

Colonel Sanders, of the Kentucky Fried Chicken franchise, began selling his chicken recipe *after he had retired.* The first hundred restaurants he went to turned him down. The next hundred turned him down. But Colonel Sanders didn't give up. He went to just about every restaurant in Tennessee. He then moved on to other states. 600 restaurants had all turned him down. When he got to the 1,000th restaurant, he was turned down again. Legend has it that Colonel Sanders sold his first deal to the 1,008th restaurant he visited.

He didn't have more time in his day than you. He simply believed in his product and put the effort of going after his dream high enough on his priority list to go out, over and over again to sell it. Your problem is not a lack of time.

Your problem is how you're utilizing your time.

Your problem is how you're utilizing your time. Your problem might be that you use your time to play video games or watch TV instead of investing in yourself and learning how to do something you love to do really well.

Zig Zigler is known as an iconic sales guru. He went all over the country, teaching people how to sell. Mr. Zigler was also known to be a very religious man. He was devoted to God and family. One day, someone challenged his teachings by means of his Christianity.

"Mr. Zigler, how do you reconcile all of that talk about money with Christianity?

Zig smiled when he answered. "It's easy. I believe God made the diamonds and put them on this earth for His crowd, not Satan's bunch."

I want you to give yourself permission to be successful. There has been a lot of differing of opinions regarding "prosperity preaching." I don't believe in that, in the sense that if I give a certain amount to a ministry, God will bless me. But I do believe that God wants His children to be successful. My Bible tells me Jacob was a millionaire. Moses was a millionaire. Solomon was the richest man who ever lived. Even Job wouldn't qualify for public assistance, if you know what I mean.

Success and money are okay, depending on what you give to get it and what you do once you've obtained it. Solomon tells us in Ecclesiastes, "He who seeks silver will never be satisfied with silver." Meaning, if money and success become a higher priority than your relationship with God to the point that it *becomes* your God, then you've got issues.

The philosophy I believe in, in terms of making money, is this: if I can help enough people get what they want, I'll be able to get everything I want.

The question I pose to you is this... what type of life do you want to live? You might find out that by shifting your priority list and by devoting maybe just forty-five minutes a day to becoming the person you want to be, in five years you can live that life or a semblance of that life. If you stay doing the same thing, you'll never be happy, never content, and never be proud of yourself.

You've got at least forty-five free minutes every day. How are you going to continue spending it?

Chapter 14

You Have to Want It

Secrets in Plain Sight

What does it take to find out how to become the best possible you? How much do you have to give of yourself to live the way God has designed for you to live? Do you think the way to becoming successful is a secret? It's not.

The first thing you need to answer is, what does success mean to you? To some, it means being in ministry. To others, it means regaining an estranged spouse and having the whole family unit together again. To many it might mean living in a mansion with expensive cars in the garage. Maybe it might mean waking up loving what you do every day to make a living. Only you can define what success means for you. The information on how to obtain a successful life is everywhere – however, maybe because you aren't looking for it, it hides in plain sight and you can't see it.

The truth is, you don't need to read this book to uncover any secrets for success. You can go online and read blogs or watch YouTube videos on how to become successful. You can take a millionaire or a mega-church pastor out to lunch and ask him or her how they managed to achieve all they've done. The methods to becoming a success are not a secret; the information is all around you. It's even in your Bible. It appears during sermons preached at your church. It's manifested every time your child hugs you.

I believe that everyone yearns to be more successful, happier, and for those who are married, to have a better relationship with their spouse. Some never find the elusive key to happiness and yet, they find themselves in the same stagnant situation as many who have. That's because many who discover how to be more successful, happier, and in a better marriage, aren't willing to put in the work required to effect that neccessary change. Because they don't want to do the work, they keep looking for an easier way, a magic wand, even though the means of living a better life is in plain sight.

They live their lives, going through the motions of looking for the answer. They desire to live better lives, but in all honesty, many have already found out how to achieve their heart's desire – but didn't like the amount of work required of them. So, they continue to search while the truth remains hidden from them... in plain sight. If you never really look for a way to be

If you never really look for a way to be better, you'll never find it.

better, you'll never find it. *Seek, and you shall find.* The secret to repairing your marriage, your relationship with your children, your pastor, your boss, or even an old classmate is out there. You just either have to look for it or, if you find it, accept the challenges that come with it and go after it.

In terms of becoming a better version of yourself, here is a truth you can't escape from – you have to want it. Not the way you might crave a Cuban sandwich, not the way you want your favorite team to win, and not even the way you want to be promoted to a new position or hired on at a new job. You have to hunger for it.

Secret to Success

Let me share with you a quick story on Socrates. He was walking along the beach with his pupil, an eager and intelligent young man.

"Master, I've been with you many years, and although you've taught me so much, I still don't know the secret to being successful."

Socrates looked at the young man and said, "Follow me."

He walked into the ocean with the young man a step behind. They walked into the water, chest deep. The young man was wondering why they were in the water, when suddenly Socrates grabbed him and pulled him under. The young man didn't struggle, he held his breath, calmly wondering what insight his master wanted to teach him. As he began to run out of oxygen, he tapped his master's hand, wanting to be let up. However, Socrates tightened his grip instead. Soon, the young man began to flail and push back against his master, fighting for his life, yet Socrates was a strong old man, and the young man stayed submerged.

The pupil struggled with all his might, realizing that if he didn't breathe soon, he would drown. At the last moment, Socrates let the young man go. The young man jumped up, taking in the deepest breaths he had ever taken in his life as his master walked to the shore.

A few minutes later, the pupil, utterly perplexed and visibly upset, reached the beach where his master stood.

"Why did you do that? Did I upset you?" he asked, as calmly as he could.

"You wanted to know the secret to success, correct?" Socrates asked.

"Yes, but…"

"When your head was under water, what was the one thing you wanted more than anything?"

"To breathe. I needed air."

Socrates began walking away, and his pupil caught up to him, still not realizing the lesson.

"When you desire to be successful, as badly as you needed to breathe, you will be successful."

That story has been told millions of times over. It's one of the go-to stories people use when writing a motivational, coaching, sales, or self-help book. The reason why it has been passed down from generation to generation is because there's truth to it.

Comfort Zone

People who desire success or change are willing to leave their comfort zones. Comfort zones are traps that prevent you from making a life instead of just making a living. You might be trapped in a comfort zone now and not even realize it.

I lived in a comfort zone for a little over twenty years, working as a corporate salesman. I always wanted more, so I would stay late, work weekends, and do whatever it took to hit my quotas. That would enable me to live the type of life I was accustomed to.

I didn't realize the amount of time my jobs were taking from my family life or from my ministry. In fact, for most of those years, I never had a ministry; I didn't think I had the time for one. When I started my own business and truly became the master of my own destiny, I realized how behind I was in many vital areas of my life.

I jumped out of my comfort zone and pressed forward, to be used by God and in my business. It amazed me how both of those areas started to take off at the same time! I later realized that, long ago, God had given me the gifts to teach, preach, and lead, but it wasn't until I moved out of my comfort zone that those gifts started to manifest themselves.

You may have heard of the story on how to boil a frog. In case you haven't heard it, I'll recap it for you. For centuries, people have said that the way you cook a frog is to put it in a pot of cool water. The frog will chill there, content. Then, you turn on the stove. Gradually, the frog feels the heat but it won't jump out of the pot. It's as if it remembers how cool the water once was and will ride out the hot water until it gets cool again. The water can start boiling and the frog will still not jump from the pot, dying there. If you were to take that same frog and try to put it in a pot full of boiling water, it would jump out immediately. In essence, it's not so much the boiling water that kills the frog, it can jump out whenever it wants, what kills it is its comfort zone.

Things might have been slipping for you for years – yet, like the frog that feels the water getting warmer, you still aren't ready to change your lifestyle, regardless of how destructive it might be. Your goals, dreams, marriage, and friendships can die if you don't get motivated to do what it takes to get out of your dysfunctional comfort zone.

Motivated people are willing to change their bedtimes, their circle of friends (if their *friends* hinder their chance for success), and even their diet. They envision a better life and realize that, if they do not change their old habits, their new life will never materialize.

Set the Pace

In 1 Samuel, Chapter 30, we read the story of when David and his men returned to their home, Ziklag. The Amalekites had invaded the south — including David's village. Their families had been smitten and homes were burned to the ground. To make matters worse, their wives, sons, and daughters had been taken captive, as slaves. Even David's two wives were taken. He was beside himself with grief.

But then something happened that distressed him even more. The people, including his men that rode with him, spoke of stoning him. The story goes on to state that David inquired of the Lord, asking, "Shall I pursue after this troop? Shall I overtake them?"

The answer? Pursue: for thou shalt surely overtake them, and without fail recover all.

David left with six hundred men, men who had all lost their families and friends. Yet, and here is why I relate this story, at some point in the journey, two hundred of the men couldn't finish the trip. The Bible says they were so faint they could not go over the brook called, Besor.

David had set such a tough pace that two hundred men like him, soldiers who had lost everything, couldn't keep up with him. They must have been so exhausted and worn out that they decided to stay by a brook instead of continuing on to free their families. While riding, each man probably thought of their wives, sons, and daughters, watching over a hill to see them arriving, and that, maybe their wives would run to tell their children, "Daddy's here. He came to save us!" However, they still couldn't keep up the pace that David had set.

Sometimes, to get the life you want, you have to be willing to do what others aren't willing or able to do. You might set a pace that is tough for you to keep up with, but manageable. However, that same pace might make people in your inner circle fall by the wayside. Some people that start off with you might drop out and leave you to go by yourself. Some people that don't even start off with you might be offended because you no longer have the time for them like you used to have. They'll think you've changed for the worse, or that you're a sell-out, that you used to be cool but now that you're in business school, you're stuck up. Don't worry about those people. They are so trapped in their comfort-zone-prisons, they'll never get it.

I imagine that David didn't stop riding when it got dark. To get what you want, to save your family or to live your dream life, you might have to be willing to set a tough pace and ride all night. You might have to push back your bedtime for study or prayer. Riding at night can get scary. You might lose your path. You might hear sounds of predators. You might ride into an ambush or, if it's dark enough, off a cliff. The bottom line is that David and 400 of his men wanted their families back so much, they were willing to do anything.

How badly do you want to change for the better? There's a difference between wanting to change and willing to do whatever it takes to change. The difference between striving for something and wanting something is that the people who strive, find a way to get there, the people that

The difference between striving for something and wanting something is that the people who strive, find a way to get there, the people that want, find a way to make excuses.

want, find a way to make excuses. My prayer is that you find the desire to have the life God has ordained for you, that you're willing to ride all night to get it.

What doesn't kill you doesn't make you stronger. Only one thing kills you. Everything else is a challenge, a test, or adversity. How you respond to challenges and adversities is what defines you.

Not Leaving This Rock

During the time when Moses led the Israelites, God told him to wipe out the inhabitants of the land He had given them. Years went by and leadership passed from Moses to Joshua. During this time, the Gibeonites were living in the land that God had given to the Israelites. When the Gibeonites heard of the victories that God had given the Israelites in Jericho and in the city of Ai, they got scared.

They sent a delegation to meet with Joshua, dressed in worn-out sacks and with old, cracked wineskins on their donkeys. They also wore worn-out sandals and old clothes. They even brought dry and moldy bread with them. They lied to Joshua and the Israel leadership and told them they came from a distant country, although they had been living in the land. They begged the Israelites to make a peace treaty with them and let them live in the land that they told them they had only recently occupied. Although, again, the Gibeonites had been living there for many years.

Joshua and the leadership did not inquire of the Lord, but instead made a peace treaty with them. Later, they discovered that they had been tricked, but allowed the peace treaty to stand because they had sworn an oath on the treaty before the Lord.

Many years later, Saul, frantically trying to regain God's favor, thought, *I'll do for God what Joshua failed to do.* He broke the covenant Joshua had established with the Gibeonites and almost succeeded in killing them all. Years after Saul's death, King David found his people suffering from a famine for what Saul did.

We all know that we reap what we sow. But have you ever come to the conclusion that sometimes, you reap what others have sown?

Maybe you're not living the life you want, not because of who you are, but because of where you come from. If you were born in a Spanish-speaking country and came to the United States as an adult without knowing the language, it's going to be extremely challenging to live the type of life you could achieve if you spoke English. Maybe you're not living the type of life you want because no one in your family had ever gone to college, so when you graduated high school, college was not an option.

That was my story for a long time.

My parents had come from Puerto Rico and answered the call to be pastors. While I was going to school and singing with the family's gospel band, it was more important to my parents for us to pray or practice music than it was for me to get good grades. When I graduated from high school with good grades, I never entertained the idea of going to college. I was forced to work in entry-level jobs: in construction, as a waiter, for moving companies, and in shipping and receiving departments, for more than twelve years after I'd graduated high school. In my case, someone very close to me told me that I had potential and got me a job in corporate sales. It was a position that only college graduates were allowed to be hired into. Based on my performance, I made a career out of it and moved up to management before I became an entrepreneur. But there was a time in my life when I would have never thought it possible to live the type of life I'm living now.

God wants you to know that He knows that you've been dealing with stuff in your life, that there's junk in your DNA that didn't begin with you. You have been handed down curses, sicknesses, or addictions that didn't start with you. The old kings and queens of your family line have caused you to have famines in different areas of your life. You didn't look for it. You didn't ask for it. You didn't want it. But you're reaping from the destructive choices your forefathers made.

Has the color of your skin held you back? Has a language barrier held you back? Has growing up in a certain area or being born to certain parents held you back? At times, we do sow what we don't reap. But you have to understand this about sowing and reaping and agriculture: those things are *seasonal*.

Where corn had been sown, grapes can later be sown. Maybe resentment was sown, or fear, or doubt, or anything that has held you back. Know that it's only for a time. You have the option of sowing more of the same negativity into yourself or of sowing something different. You can bring rain to where there's a drought in your life.

Let's get back to David and the famine Saul sowed unto him.

To make amends, David asked the Gibeonites how he could atone for the sins of Saul. They asked for seven of Saul's male sons to be handed to them. David ordered a decree and seven of Saul's sons were handed over to the Gibeonites. Two of the men taken were sons of a woman called Rizpah, who was one of Saul's concubines. The Gibeonites went outside where they lived and hung the seven men, killing them. The famine ended, but the story didn't, not for Rizpah.

Can you imagine how Rizpah must have felt? Her only sons were killed because of something they did not do. They were killed because of the sins of their father.

God might be telling you that it's time to release what happened to you in the past, in order to have a brighter future. There is no way your latter days will be better than your past if you continue to let the sorrows of the past affect your present. There is no way to alter the

There is no way to alter the trajectory of your life if your present doesn't change.

trajectory of your life if your present doesn't change. Only by changing your present mindset can you have a better life. As for Rizpah, although her sons were dead, she was not finished with being a protective mother.

2 Samuel 21:10

"Rizpah daughter of Aiah took sackcloth and spread it out for herself on a rock. From the beginning of the harvest, till the rain poured down from the heavens on the bodies, she did not let the birds touch them by day or the wild animals by night."

Rizpah, a former concubine, which meant that she lived in the lap of luxury in the palace, took a sackcloth and spread it over a rock. The Bible doesn't state how long she was there, but a period of days or weeks passed before the bodies were brought down. During that time, the Bible states she did not let the birds touch them by day or the wild animals by night.

If God thought it important enough to let us know that, we need to understand that during the day, birds of prey came to nibble and bite on the bodies of her sons and she shooed them off. During the dead of night, this woman – not trained in warfare and most likely not having a sword, spear, or shield – protected the bodies of her sons from the wild animals at night.

Can you imagine how scared Rizpah must have been when she heard the growl of a lion or a leopard at night? Regardless of how scared she might have felt on the inside, the wild animals that came for her sons found themselves face to face with a woman who did not have an inch of give-up in her.

What also calls my attention about this story is that she chose to sleep on a rock. Surely, she could have laid her sackcloth on the ground or somewhere more comfortable. I believe that she slept on a rock because she didn't want to get too comfortable. If she got too comfortable, she could have fallen into a deep sleep and not heard the quiet steps of an approaching predator.

At times, to change, you're going to be uncomfortable. It feels weird to do something new and to try to think differently than you have your whole life. If taking a night class is new, it's going to be uncomfortable. You're going to have to readjust the way your life was to the way your life will be for a certain amount of time in order for your life to get to where you want it to be afterward.

Living up to your calling, living up to your destiny, living the life you desire does not come easy. You have to want it badly. You have to be willing to ride all night for it. And you have to be willing to protect it. Rizpah was there when they cut her sons down and she buried them with respect, honor, and dignity. Don't leave your rock, regardless of how uncomfortable it might make you. Don't live for the present; live your present to live a better future.

Chapter 15

Seismic Shifts

Let the Dry Land Appear

A seismic shift is what causes earthquakes. Enormous rocks or clumps of hardened earth, called plates, that stretch many miles long, sometimes even thousands of miles, sit miles beneath the surface. When the rocks move or shift, the earth quakes.

When God first created the earth, the exterior was all water. In Chapter 2 we see that the Spirit of God moved upon the face of the waters. But, in verse 9 we read that God says, "Let the waters under the heavens be gathered together unto one place, and let the dry land appear: and it was so.

I believe when God said *let the dry land appear*, massive seismic shifts took place under the earth and solid ground appeared, displacing the water that was once there, forcing it to become one. In order for it to become one, other seismic shifts happened and the earth fell upon itself, creating massive chasms deep enough to hold the oceans and rivers on the planet. I believe it was those seismic shifts that happened long ago that formed the continents as they are.

I believe that we are products of our own seismic shifts. Things, events, spoken words, done or said to us years ago make up who we are today, how we think, and how we react. These shifts most likely happened at a time when our minds were vulnerable or still developing, much like the earth was when God created it. They have created a pattern that perhaps you don't like, but you can't get away from.

I have spent time on this book trying to get you to ascertain whether or not you need to change your mindset. I would be remiss if I were to finish this book without delivering to you some new ways of thinking or some truths that could replace the thoughts that have brought you to a place where you experience discontent with your present life.

Winners Think Differently

We love winners. It's in our nature. If you meet a famous person – athlete, coach, actor, singer, whatever, you would most likely want to take a picture with that person and upload it to your social media feeds. You wouldn't feel the same way about the average Joe that sits next to you on a plane. Why? Because we love winners.

The reason why some people are winners is mainly because of their mindset. Great preachers don't captivate large audiences because they love to talk. They're great preachers because they have spent time in the Word and, when they started preaching, they critiqued themselves and got better at making their points. Ask any great preacher how they did in their first sermon and they'll tell you they stuttered and stammered throughout most of it. If you consider them great, it's probably because they worked at it. If they worked at it, it's because of the mindset they have.

Winners hang out together. They eat together. They play golf together. They congregate together. Winners are fond of interacting with each other whether they are corporate winners, athletic winners, artistic winners or spiritual winners. Oh yes, even spiritual winners gravitate to other spiritual winners. Winners don't care what nationality a person is or how much money they have, they will spend time and take selfies with someone else if they consider that person to be a winner in their respective field. Even though they may make a living in different ways, in a way, they feel connected, a kinship, if you will, because they know what it takes to be a winner.

Winners, for the most part, have the same mentality. They are laser-focused. Their priority lists are similar, even though they live different lives. At the top of their priority lists is, "How can I get even better?" Professional athletes don't gain fifty pounds of fat in the off-season, they work on getting better. Even the highest paid actors still have acting coaches. The top singers have singing coaches. The top executives have business coaches.

Winners don't bother with foolishness. Once you develop that type of mentality, you can hear someone talk for two minutes and your mind is made up, because either it has fed you or it hasn't. If it hasn't, you don't bother arguing or correcting the person. You just sort of shuffle on by and go on your way. You don't mess with foolishness because they run counter to where you are trying to go. Winners don't get sidetracked or blown off course, they keep moving forward.

If you pick up any newspaper at any given time, you might read about a company that was making millions of dollars and now is going out of business. Years later the people that opened that business open a similar one under a new name and the new business also makes millions of dollars. You might see someone who had it all, lost it, gets it all back, loses it again, and gets it all back again five or six times. All the while you're struggling to have it all just one time and this person is playing with success like a yoyo. You might stare at him from the sidelines and ask, *how can he do that?* It's because he has a winner's mentality and a winner's attitude. It doesn't mean he wins all the time, it means his losses don't change his mindset.

Likewise, losers have their own clique. They're quick to blame, quick to quit, quick to dismiss new ideas, and slow to take good advice. The loser culture is so strong, a notorious winner can get around failing people, ingest their negativity and not find himself able to get back up again. There are many stories of successful people who do drugs and eventually lose it all. Most homeless people were not born homeless. But when everyone around you is down, everything you hear is gloom, and you can't get away from the losers that opine about you and your circumstances, your mentality produces a seismic shift and the earthquake tears down the confidence you once had in yourself and in God.

Not everyone is called to pastor, to become evangelists, to become prophets, or Bible teachers. Yes, we are all called to spread the Good News, but we are all called to do it differently. One brother can be called to be a pastor, while another brother who loves the Lord just as much is called to become a business owner, and through his tithings and giving their offering, pastors would most likely lose their churches. How can a church positively impact a community if the parishioners have nowhere to congregate? He will help finance the Kingdom of God on earth. Before you theologians get on my case, yes, I know that God is the owner of all silver and gold. But let's be honest, if everyone at your church stopped tithing and offerings, how can your church impact or serve the community if the parishioners have no way to congregate? God doesn't need the money, but we on earth do.

As a ghostwriter, I've had the honor and privilege to write books for many people. Usually, my clients are people that have achieved a very high level of success, either in their ministry or their business. After spending hours upon hours of time with them... interviewing them, collaborating with them, and gaining their knowledge and insight to where I can write a book as if I were them, I've picked up quite a few things about a winner's mentality. Here are some thoughts that winners share. I pray they enter your very bloodstream and every time your heart beats, it beats with the rhythm of a winner.

Winners are ambitious. Ambition is not a bad thing, as money is not evil. It's when you love money more than your relationship with God that money becomes a problem. Ambition becomes bad when one is willing to rob, steal, and cheat anyone in order to get ahead. But when ambition spurs on an inner drive that propels you forward, regardless of the circumstances, I would go as far to say, it's a God thing!

Winners take responsibility. No one else. Take responsibility for it and, if you need to make a change, make the necessary changes, just don't blame anyone else for your situation.

Wherever you are in life, high or low, you got yourself there.

right people.

Winners are always willing to learn. Wherever you are in life, high or low, you got yourself there. They are always students and always coachable by the

Winners have faith. Some might call it being optimistic or having positive thinking, but I call it having faith that, with everything the enemy planned to do to destroy you, God will use those circumstances to help you.

Winners are humble. They don't let their ego get in the way of their success. It's hard for someone else to say how great you are if you're constantly tooting your own horn. Everyone doesn't need to know about all your accolades, anyway. In fact, many winners end up dismissing their accolades many years later. That's because they have grown so much since that time and have reached even higher levels. So, for them to be reminded of something others might find amazing, to them it's not a full compliment, it's mildly belittling because it reminds them of a time when they weren't as good as they later became.

Winners are passionate. They love what they do and they're passionate about life. People follow passionate people. It's their passion that draws others into their goals and dreams and convinces other people to give their time, energy, and intelligence to feed that person's dreams.

Winners are self-motivated. They don't only put in work when others can see them. They'll get up early and stay up late doing what needs to be done. They don't need pep talks or a cheering section. They have a permanent fire that burns inside them. That fire glows hot whether they're in public or in private.

Spiritual winners do all those things for Christ. They're ambitious to do God's will. They take it as their responsibility to show others the love of God or to be a Good Samaritan to strangers. Faith comes through hearing of the Word, so they are always willing to learn more about God. Some don't get enough sermons on Sundays, so they watch Christian programming or YouTube videos of their favorite preachers. They'll even sign up for academic studies, Bible colleges, or Bible institutes. They have faith that, regardless of the situation, God will see them through. And they are passionate about following Jesus and pleasing him, even if it means denying themselves physical or earthly pleasures.

Toll Road

Have you ever been on a toll road long enough that you were surprised when you had to stop at a toll booth and pay? Don't get too excited because you got on that road free. Sooner or later, if you want to get from one destination to another, you're going to have to pay the price. You don't get to ride toll roads free of charge.

Have you ever seen a couple interact? By "couple," I mean a pair that has been married for many years. It seems like they understand each other so well. If you go to their house you probably feel a sense of peace and understanding. In your naivety, you might even say to one or both of them, "I wish I had a marriage like yours."

Don't let the palm leaves fool you, that couple had been riding a toll road for a long time. If they have been together for twenty, thirty, forty, or even fifty years, they've paid a price for it. Perhaps pots and pans used to fly between them, perhaps very bad things were said to each other, perhaps family members or friends had gotten in between them for a time, perhaps there were doors slammed and someone went to live at his or her mom's house for a while. The truth is, they have paid a price for the peace you experience when you visit them. It takes more than just time to gel with someone so well you barely have to speak to communicate.

In the same way, to get from where you are to where you want to get to, you're going to have to go through the toll road. You're going have to pay in some way: money, loss of friendships, free time, hobbies, sleep, or something else you hold dear. A very successful businessman once said to me, "Eli, it's not getting to the destination that's the problem, it's being willing to lose what you have to in order to get there."

I don't know what you're going to have to pay to get to where God is calling you. But I do know that it's not going to kill you. I do know that whatever it is, you have the ability to pay it. The future God has for you is worth the price He requires you to pay.

Chapter 16

Temporary over Permanent

Hangry

When you were a child, did you ever want something so badly that if you didn't get it, you thought it would ruin your life or you'd die? Maybe you got it, maybe you didn't. One thing I can tell you, if you didn't get it, most likely it didn't ruin your life and it certainly didn't kill you.

There's a slang word: *Hangry.* Have you heard it? Basically, it depicts that you get uncommonly angry and the anger stems from being hungry. They took the words *hungry* and *angry* and merged them to come up with *hangry.* It sort of gives you a pass when you're acting obnoxious because you are hungry. Mars, the Snickers bar company, has a series of commercials regarding people not acting like themselves because they are hungry. In the commercial, when the person gets a Snickers bar, they resort to their normal self.

The commercial might appear as a new thought and the word *hangry* might appear like something new, but people have been acting outside of their character when they've been hungry since, well... forever. In fact, there's an article entitled, *Why do I get Hangry,* published on Time Magazine's online portal, www.time.com on August 26, 2015, by Markham Heid that proves the medical and scientific truth to hangry-ness. In the article, Dr.

Brad Bushman, a professor of psychology at Ohio State University states that people commonly feel an uptick in anger or aggression when they're hungry. "The brain needs fuel to regulate emotions, and anger is the emotion people have the most difficulty regulating," he explains. This explains what happened to Esau way back in the Old Testament days.

Genesis 25: 29-33

"29 And Jacob sod pottage: and Esau came from the field, and he was faint:

30 And Esau said to Jacob, Feed me, I pray thee, with that same red pottage; for I am faint: therefore was his name called Edom.

31 And Jacob said, Sell me this day thy birthright.

32 And Esau said, Behold, I am at the point to die: and what profit shall this birthright do to me?

33 And Jacob said, Swear to me this day; and he sware unto him: and he sold his birthright unto Jacob."

In this passage, we can clearly see that Esau is not feeling like himself. Esau is the first-born, the one who will be given everything his father owns. By the way, their father Isaac was one of the wealthier men in the area at the time. Jacob, who was born mere seconds after Esau, knew that when their father died, he was going to be left with nothing. So, he did something about it.

When Esau came in from the fields, Jacob had made a stew. I can imagine that the aroma of the stew filled up the tent or house when Esau entered. He was hungry and wanted it badly, so badly he thought it would ruin his life if he didn't get it, worse yet, he thought he would die if he didn't get it.

We know that Esau was a hunter, thus more than likely he was a strong young man. I wasn't there, but I believe that Esau had enough energy to make a stew of his own. They had servants, so Esau could have had someone make him it. Being that they were rich, there was probably some bread or something he could have munched on while it was being made for him. Esau's problem was that he was a brat.

The way he asked for the stew is telling of his personality. It appears that he was used to getting what he asked for. When he asked for it, he said he's about to pass out. A little dramatic, don't you think? Jacob offered a deal, "I'll give you the stew if you give me your birthright."

Esau basically said, "My birthright means nothing to me at this time. The only thing I want is something to eat!"

Jacob couldn't believe it and pressed the issue. "Swear to me that I can have your birthright."

Esau looked at Jacob, nostrils filled with the aroma of the stew, "I swear brother, if you give me some of your stew, I'll give you my birthright."

Esau ate the stew and got full. Jacob ended up living his life the same way a millionaire would today. It wasn't supposed to be that way. We will never know if it was God that induced a deep hunger into Esau or if it wasn't His plan at all and that the free will that He gave Esau bypassed His sovereign plan for him. The fact remains that the family dynamic was thrown out of balance. We do know that it didn't play out the way Isaac had wanted it. My reason for bringing up this story is to tell you this – Esau ruined his future when he made a permanent decision over a temporary situation.

Some people will say that Esau was *hangry* or that he made a bad choice. I don't think so. I think it goes deeper than that. I think Esau was just a stupid, pompous, brat. He should have known what his birthright meant. He should have known he wouldn't have fainted without the stew. The Bible doesn't say he was brought in on a cot because he was dying of starvation. Esau the hunter walked into the house on his own volition and stupidly traded away his inheritance.

Some people get stuck on stupid and never realize it. There are men that have been married for fifteen years and still don't know when their wife's birthday is or when their anniversary is. It's true. Let's look into that for a moment. If a husband forgot to get his wife a gift on her birthday or their anniversary, she'd say something to him. Most likely she yelled at him or she cried and told him how she couldn't believe he forgot her birthday, probably again.

Yet, fifteen years later, if you ask the husband to name the date of his wife's birthday or their anniversary, he won't know! That's not someone who just doesn't care. Because whether he cared or not, he would have heard the date over and over again. That guy is just stuck on stupid.

Earlier in this book, I talked about people who've been stuck in the same rut for the last five years. The truth of the matter is that some people have been stuck on the same stupid their father died of. There's probably a more *Christian* way to say it but some people need to be told that they've been stuck on stupid and it's time to smarten up.

Genesis 37: 34

"And when Esau heard the words of his father, he cried with a great and exceeding bitter cry, and said unto his father, Bless me, even me also, O my father."

The Bible says Esau repented. He wanted to take back the trade he had made with his brother. It says he cried with a great and exceedingly bitter cry. There's no doubt that the man lamented his decision and was suffering. He realized at that moment how the rest of his life was going to be.

But Esau is not the only person that has made a permanent decision over a temporary situation. There are people in prisons all over the world for something they've done on the spur of the moment. There are many people that are divorced for what was done or said during a temporary situation. There are many people who've lost great jobs for acting out during a temporary situation. Friendships have been irrevocably damaged from something decided at the spur of a moment.

Esau cried real tears. He got emotional. He repented for what he had done. But he didn't change. Many people who go to church believe that when they hear a sermon and go for prayer, it's going to mean change. They leave their seats and, with as much reverence as they can muster, they walk to the pulpit, they pray or get prayed over, and they cry. They repent. They get emotional. But oftentimes it doesn't result in change. Emotions are temporary. You might be happy right now, but two hours from now you may hear some bad news and your mood will change. People in churches all across the globe believe that if they go up to the front for prayer, they are going to change.

The problem is, they're the ones who continue to come to the front. They're the ones who continue to repent. They're the ones who continue to get prayed for. I don't want to minimize the effect of prayer and I don't want to minimize how great it is to be influenced by the Holy Spirit to repent. That's powerful. And if all you want to do is to leave church feeling good, keep doing that. But if you want God to help you change, you can't rely on temporary emotions, you're going to have to shift your mindset.

Software programs have a default setting. You can open a Microsoft Word document and change the font and write an entire book in that font. You can even change the language and write your book in Spanish or Russian if you like. But open up your Word program again and it reverts back to its default font and language.

Many people are like that. When they go to church or church-related events, they change their font. They change the way they talk and how they act. But when they go home, they go back to their default settings. Too many of us in this fallen world are not sure what our default setting is. We have been using another font for so long that it looks weird when we use the font we started with.

The Moment of Truth

A pig and a sheep can fall into the same pit of mud. The difference is the pig is programmed to like the mud but the sheep isn't. The sheep looks around and comes to a moment of truth. It says to itself, "What am I doing here? I don't belong in this mess!"

The sheep will cry, kick, and scream because it knows it wasn't made to wallow in the mud like a pig. Hours, and even days later it will continue to cry out for help. It was made for open air and high ground, not to be stuck in the mud.

If there are areas of your life that are a mess, I pray that I'm giving you the tools to get yourself out of it. For many people, they need to believe that they can get out of it. God's people have help, we have faith.

You might say to yourself, "There's no way I can change my lifestyle."

Faith will tell you, "This was never meant to be my lifestyle. With God's help, I know I can find the person I was meant to be."

You might say to yourself, "The situation I'm in is too hard."

Faith will tell you, "Don't you remember all the things God has already gotten you through? What's this one little thing?"

As a man thinketh, so is he. The question of whether or not you can or will change depends on what you think about yourself. So, what are you, a pig or a sheep? A pig belongs in the mud. A sheep belongs in a flock... where it can be pastored.

Chapter 17

What Now?

In the Still of the Night

While I was going through my radiation and chemotherapy treatment, I was often on some sort of pain medicine. But I still remember one night vividly, even though I was on medication. It was nearly 3:00 a.m. and my throat was in a tremendous amount of pain. I had vomited about thirty minutes prior and my stomach was threatening to unleash a nasty dry-heave session against me. It was early Sunday morning – for me, still Saturday night.

I remember this night clearly because it was the only time I really felt like giving up. I didn't want to throw up anymore. I didn't want to *just barely* sleep again. I was sick of tossing and turning and suffering from pain. I did not want to wake up the next day and go through the same routine as the day before. I was tapped out.

I had lost twenty-five pounds in less than five weeks. I had been hospitalized for a week with a blood infection. I had to put ice bags under my armpits to break free from a fever. I couldn't eat. I couldn't speak. I could barely walk. I was just fed up with it all. My weak body grabbed at my weak spirit and held it, tight.

That's it, God. I'm okay if you take me. I don't want to live another day like today. Just… take me.

I tried to sleep with the thought of my death on my mind, believing it to be a comforting thought. I wanted God to take me while I slept. I wanted to wake up in His arms, pain and worry free. It seemed like the best option for me. I knew my death would cause my loved ones pain, but I'd lived a good fifty years, something that many people hadn't been fortunate enough to do. As I tried to drift off to what I was hoping was my final slumber with that thought on my mind, another thought snuck in.

If this was my last day, can I honestly say I lived a good life?

I thought of who I was – a husband to an amazing wife, a father to five children, whom I loved dearly and who loved me, the son of Reverend Jesus and Digna Gonzalez, a brother to my siblings, a grandfather to two beautiful kids, and a friend to too many to count. Yes, I'd lived a good life. Not a perfect life, but a life filled with laughter and love. I was even more prepared for God to take me.

A few hours later I woke up from sleep with pain and I reflected on what I had done with my time here on earth. That thought interrupted my peace with dying that night. I tried to shake it out of my head because I didn't like the answer that was forming in my subconscious. But it nagged at me and forced me to consider it.

If this was my last day, can I be proud of what I've done?

I looked back on my ministry and I didn't like what I saw. I believed God had bestowed gifts upon me that I'd never maximized. The prophetic word over my life, spoken many years ago when I was running away from the Lord, had never been fulfilled. I didn't blame it on God for lying to me, I blamed it on myself for allowing my will to take me out of God's plan.

I thought of my business, and again I was left wanting. I had only been writing for five years. Yes, I had written more than eighty books for others in that short time frame, but why had I waited so long to start? I started thinking of the hours I had spent in front of the television – easily four or five hours a night, just about every night. I thought about the times I'd spent frivolously. The hours I had spent playing mindless games on my phone. I thought of my willingness to put things off for another day... things that I should have done that day.

Suddenly, I wasn't sure I wanted God to take me. I wanted a second chance. I wanted to recommit to Him. I wanted another opportunity to bend my will to please Him. I wanted more time to build a legacy for my children and grandchildren. I wanted to see my sons and daughters marry. I wanted to... I wanted to live. Badly.

In the dead of night, I lay on the hospital bed in the dark. My throat wouldn't allow me to speak out loud so I *thought* a prayer to God.

Father God, thank you for giving me the gift of life. Thank you for allowing me to be born into the family I was born into. Thank you for my wife, for my children, my grandchildren, my brothers and sisters, my friends, and for my church family.

Lord, I'm so sorry. I'm sorry for wasting so much of the time You have given me. I don't know what Your plan is, but I know that thousands have died from what I'm going through. I pray that it be Your will that I be allowed to live more days on this earth. If it's Your will that this sickness take me, I pray that You reconsider.

Please, Lord, allow me more days of life. I promise not to squander them. I promise to dedicate them to You. I promise to live the kind of life You want me to. I beg you, Lord, let me see the light of day tomorrow. Help me beat this thing that afflicts me. Don't let it be the end of me. I have too much work to do for You. I have too much to build so that my family is taken care of. I thank You in advance because I know one day soon, I'll be standing on my own strength. I'll be speaking about Your greatness, and I'll be doing the work I should have been doing all along.

The next morning, the light of day had filled my hospital room. I was no longer afraid of the cancer. Nor was I planning on dying any time soon. My heart was filled with a peace I had never felt before. Even though I'd passed another painful day, I knew each day I suffered was getting me closer to that time when I would stop suffering.

That night, before going to bed, God put it in my heart to write this book. It was about 3:00 a.m. Monday morning – still Sunday night to me – and while in the hospital, I had finished what became chapters 8 and 11. Chapter 8, *Makes You Stronger* – was my declaration that cancer was not going to kill me. Chapter 11, *Bones of Praise* – was my way of praising God for what He was about to do in my life.

It's Up to You

I heard someone say a while ago, that it's up to each of us to take personal responsibility for his or her personal growth. I can't recall where I heard it. It could have been from one of the many business seminars I've attended or one of the many sermons I've heard. While I can't give credit to whoever said it, I can pass it along to you. You need to command ownership of your personal growth.

Living the life you are called to live is up to no one but you.

Making your spouse fall madly in love with you, again, is up to no one but you.

Having a prayer life is up to no one but you.

Instructing your children in the ways of the Lord is up to no one but you.

Putting in the work to advance in your job is up to no one but you.

Whether you decide to start your own business is up to no one but you.

Whether you live in paradise with the King for eternity is up to no one but you.

In the first chapter of this book, I asked you to agree with me that better days are ahead of you, that whatever good or bad you did in the past is in the past, and that God's grace is sufficient to always love you and continue to forgive you. Now, I lay down a challenge: are you going to do what it takes to ensure that better days are ahead for you? Will you take ownership of your spiritual and personal growth?

Why Are You Walking?

My father would often tell a story about how an eagle's egg wound up in a chicken coop. When the egg hatched, the baby eagle saw himself surrounded by chickens, so he thought he was a chicken. He quickly grew much bigger than the chickens and thought something was wrong, but didn't know what. He had trouble fitting in and, to make matters worse, the chickens had started to tease and bully him.

One particular time, a bunch of chickens were chasing him to beat him up. As he ran, he flapped his wings for balance and something incredible happened. He started to fly!

When he was in the air, he saw another eagle. That eagle said to him, "I was wondering how long you were going to hang out with those chickens. Nothing against chickens but, why walk when you can fly?"

I'd like you to understand that at the very moment you were saved, every gift from God became available to you. Yet, spiritually, you may have been living with a semblance of fear. You may have been walking with regret and being shamed by guilt. Perhaps you have continuously tripped on your path over and over again, never realizing that you were walking down a path that is foreign to you... because it was not meant for you. Maybe you have not reached spiritual maturity, even though you have as much access to God and His supernatural favor as any other human on earth.

You may have been waiting for church to bring a sick family member so a pastor or minister could pray for them. Let me remind you, there is no pastor, no prophet, no teacher, and no minister that has more access to God than you. We may have different callings, but we each have equal access to God's blessings, healings, forgiveness, and mercy.

Free yourself from any self-imposed bondage, from any self-imposed limits to your spiritual, financial, or mental growth. You are the head, not the tail. You are an eagle, not a chicken.

Once you realize you can fly, you'll never walk again.

A Better Life Awaits

It's never the perfect time to implement change. Today is as good as any. There's a saying: *You only live once.* I disagree with it, vehemently. I'd rather live knowing that I'll only die once but that I get to live every single day God grants me.

Hopefully, you don't have to nearly die from cancer or another illness to fully appreciate the gift of life. You're on a path, whether you realize it or not. You might be on a path to nowhere or somewhere. If you don't better yourself in any area of your life, you're on a path to nowhere. You're stagnant. You're stuck. You may as well be paralyzed. However, if you're on the move, figure out where you're headed.

Don't mistake movement for progress. Make sure you know where your path leads. There is a path that leads to spiritual wellness, emotional wellness, and financial wellness. Don't be fooled into

Don't mistake movement for progress.

thinking that you can only have an abundance of only one of those.

This part of our journey together has come to an end. I've got but a few words left for you here. If you'd like to invite me to your church or group to speak, please check out the *About the Author* section to see how to get in touch with me.

Remember, when all else is falling apart around you, raise your hands and give God praise. Let Him handle what He needs to handle, but then make sure to do what's in your control to do.

The foundation has been laid. A seed has been deposited in your mind and spirit. I'm excited for the new, better you that's about to emerge. You deserve to live a life full of love, good health, peace, joy, and prosperity... just like God intended.

About the Author

Eli "Che" Gonzalez was born to Rev. Jesus and Digna Gonzalez in Rochester, New York in 1968. He lived most of his life in Milford, MA, where he went to school and sang with the family gospel band, The Gonzalez Brothers. He currently resides in the Tampa Bay area with his beautiful wife, Maria, and their daughter Trinity. His life is almost complete when his other children, Joshua, Mia, Alexis, and Isaiah come to visit.

As a ghostwriter, Eli has written more than eighty books for others, many of which have earned legitimate Best Seller status. He is the President and Senior Writer of The Ghost Publishing. In 2017, Eli founded the International Ghostwriter's Association. The IGA provides the only online course that trains and certifies ghostwriters.

On a professional level, Eli has served as a keynote speaker at some of the largest business or publishing conferences in the country. He also serves as an advisor to the Board of Directors for the Hispanic Chamber of Commerce, Tampa Bay, Florida.

On a ministry-level, Eli is a registered evangelist in good standing with Trayendo Esperanza. He is a sought-after preacher and has ghostwritten Christian books for ministry leaders known all over the world.

To reach out to Eli Gonzalez to speak at an event, you can reach him at:

Email: Eli@theghostpublishing.com

Twitter: @EliGhost1

When Eli is not writing, working, or preaching, he can be found walking on a beach in the Sunshine State alongside his wife and life-mate, enjoying another day God has given him.

Acknowledgments

First and foremost, I'd like to thank God, the Father, Jesus, the Son, and the Holy Spirit for finding me when I was lost. Thank You for giving me purpose and destiny. Thank you for Your mercy and grace. And thank You for allowing me more days on this earth.

My wife, Maria "Malinda" Gonzalez. I can never thank you enough for your unconditional love. Ever since I met you, and you fell in love with me ☺, you have never wavered on your love and commitment to our family and me. You are my rock and I'm more than blessed to call you my wife. I love you with my life.

Joshua, Mia, Alexis, Isaiah, and Trinity. My starting five. Thank you, although you probably don't know it, but you push me to make something out of myself, so that you can be proud of me and so I can set the right example. I love you each – THE SAME! I don't have a favorite, so stop asking! ☺

Reverend Jesus "Chuito" and Digna Gonzalez, my awesome and amazing parents. Thanks for teaching me about God's love ever since I was born. Thanks for being role models and for never giving up on me.

Jessie "Big J" – Orlando "Truck" – Marylin "Mama" – Sorines "Titi Soly" – Steven "the white boy of the family" – Herson – "Heavy" and Benjamin "Benny" - - - I am who I am mainly because of your influences in my life. Being your brother is one of the things I am most proud of. I love you guys so much.

Peter Lopez – my "ride or die" brother, my best friend, my calm in many storms. Thanks for teaching me how to think and speak life. Your confidence in me and my abilities have propelled me to live a much better life. Our brotherhood will never be shaken.

Maria Esquilin – my mother-in-law whom I call, "Mom." Thank you for accepting me with open arms from the beginning. You've been with me through the good and bad. Thanks for your prayers, your hospitality, your wisdom, and your kindness. Like you, there is none other.

Joe and Sandy Lugo – my brother and sister-in-law from my wife's side. You were my pastors for more than ten years. I learned so much and grew so much under your covering. Thanks for the love and support throughout all these years, even though at times I didn't make it easy. I love that we are family.

Yazmin, Natty, Santiago, Julie, Valerie, and Lisa – my brothers and sisters-in-law from my side. I have a special place in my heart for each of you. From eating at Yazmin's kitchen to being grabbed by Natty, to partying back in the day with Santiago, to being roommates with Julie – and after that to her having a key to my apartment so she could make a ham and cheese while going from college to work, to watching Valerie, in awe on how you translate messages – including your own, to cracking up at Lisa's humor and marveling at your incredible memory. I love each and every one of you.

My many nieces and nephews. There are literally more than forty of you, so I won't name you all. Just know that Tio Che loves you.

Acknowledgments

Pastor David and Aida Rivera – it's an honor to be a member of your church. Thanks for accepting my family and for seeing the calling God has on our lives.

Pastor David Jr. and Jessica Rivera – we are with you 100% as you embark on establishing Restore Family Church. We have bonded quickly in such a short amount of time. David Jr., you are one of the best preachers I've heard. Jessica, you're just a little crazy, but totally awesome. We love you.

Members of Iglesia de Dios Pentecostal, M.I. – Church Ave, Tampa. The outpouring of love and respect you have afforded us is astounding. I want to name some names so badly but I know I'm going to miss some so I'll just thank you as a whole. To the many people that called my wife during my sickness, the leaders of each church group that gave us a love offering, and to the pastors and ministers – we love you all and consider ourselves privileged to congregate and worship the Lord alongside you.

Members of Countryside Español – we have been family since I first walked in. It amazes me that my wife and I are the godparents to five beautiful children within that ministry. Alex, Jesus, Martha, Reymir, Khyrsis... the list goes on and on. I can't tell you how much we miss and love you.

Eli Gonzalez Facebook Group – to all of you who have followed my journey and have encouraged me along the way, I thank you for being there for me. You have inspired me more than you'll ever know, to not only get through cancer, but to make something great out of my life. I plan on never losing touch with you all.

Big Bob Puntonio – my best friend from way, way back. Thanks for your unwavering friendship. We've been through a lot and we're still mad tight. I love you, bro.

Darlene and Joe Stevenson – I met Joe at the basketball courts and didn't like him at first because he kept raining jumpers on me. Darlene and Maria worked together and then Darlene became her supervisor and helped Maria advance to also become a supervisor. We all got together and everything just clicked. Thanks for your friendship, for coming to visit me in the hospital and for dropping off those delicious mashed potatoes when that was all I could eat.

TGP Team – Herson Gonzalez, Lil Barcaski, Janice Chico, Lisa Walls, William Walls, Christine James, Linda Hinkle, and Becky Lee – thanks for sharing in my vision and for blending in your talents and gifts into making TGP the premiere ghostwriting team in the country.

Love you Rosie. Edvin, I appreciate our conversations, Joey, can't wait to see your boy, and Dennis – the DNA results are in – I AM YOUR GODFATHER!

Dr. Larry Keefauver – thanks for seeing something in me and agreeing to work with me. I value your ministry and your knowledge.

To you, dear reader - Whether you know me or not, thanks for taking the time to read this book. I pray that it has strengthened your faith and your resolve in living the type of life God has designed for you to live. Go after your dream life – hard. Go after it with all you have. It's worth it.

Acknowledgments

To the many Cancer Survivors – let's not use the word remission. That denotes that it might come back. Use the word healed or cured. I'm humbled to be one of you. Many of you have gone through far worse than I. You are true heroes and I admire your courage and strength. I hope that you share your story and inspire others. I also urge you to fight every day to live the life you have always wanted to live. You have been granted one more shot on this earth. Make yourself and your families proud. God loves you.

My kids and grandson invading the waiting area during my first radiation treatment.

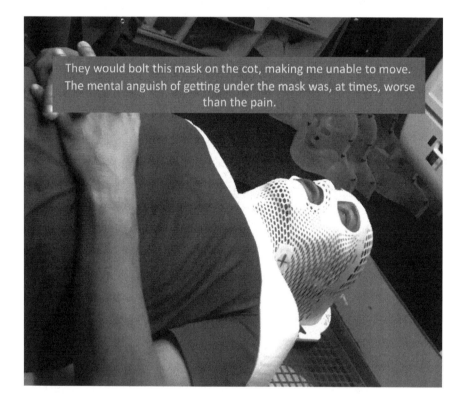

They would bolt this mask on the cot, making me unable to move. The mental anguish of getting under the mask was, at times, worse than the pain.

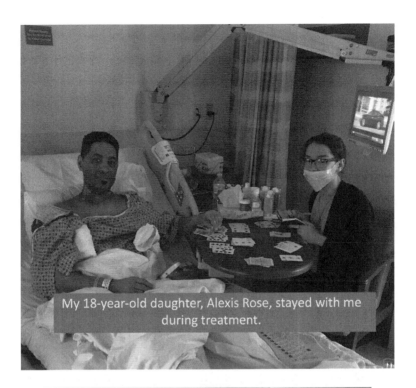

My 18-year-old daughter, Alexis Rose, stayed with me during treatment.

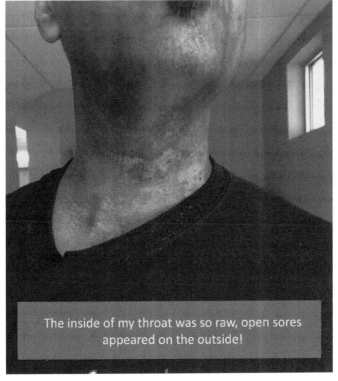

The inside of my throat was so raw, open sores appeared on the outside!

Sleeping in Maria's bed - I would sleep with the vomit bag directly under my mouth.

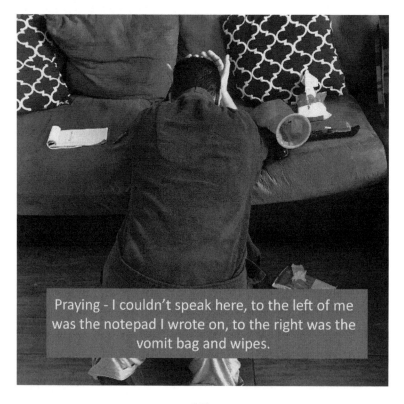

Praying - I couldn't speak here, to the left of me was the notepad I wrote on, to the right was the vomit bag and wipes.

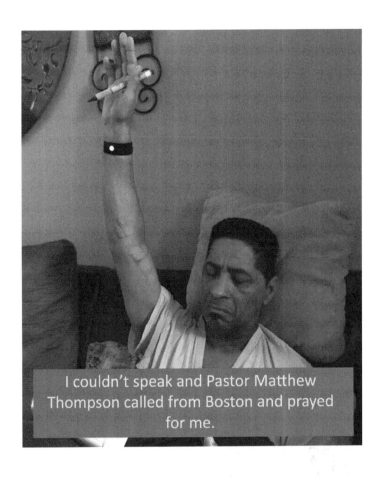

I couldn't speak and Pastor Matthew Thompson called from Boston and prayed for me.

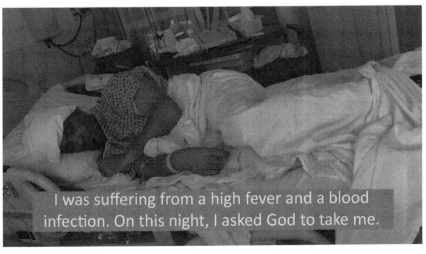

I was suffering from a high fever and a blood infection. On this night, I asked God to take me.

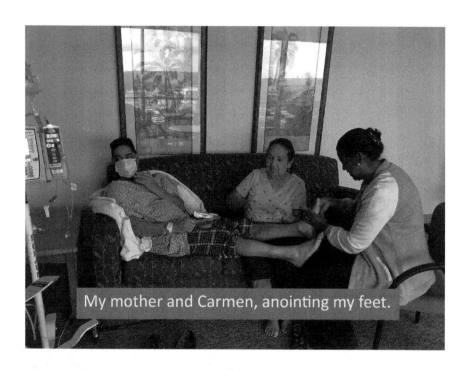

My mother and Carmen, anointing my feet.

My wife, brother-in-law, mother-in-law, and family friend celebrating my last day of radiation.

Healed from Cancer. At TD Jakes' Pastors & Leadership Conference